FREEDOM

Freedom

Battle Strategies for Conquering Temptation

Everett Fritz

Foreword by Jason Evert

Ignatius Press–Lighthouse Catholic Media

San Francisco   DeKalb, Illinois

Ignatius Press Distribution
P.O. Box 1339
Fort Collins, CO 80522
Tel: (800) 651-1531
www.ignatius.com

Lighthouse Catholic Media
733 Enterprise Avenue
DeKalb, IL 60115
Tel: (866) 767-3155
www.lighthousecatholicmedia.org

Cover Design by Christopher Murphy

Contents

Foreword

By Jason Evert

A young man once told me that although he was sleeping with his girlfriend, he loved her so much that he would die for her.

"Really?" I asked him, "You'd die for her?"

"Yep. If someone took a gun and put it to her head, I'd tell him to shoot me instead."

"No kidding," I remarked, "you'd take a bullet for her?"

"Absolutely."

"Alright then," I said. "If you're willing to die for her, then do it."

With a bewildered expression on his face, he asked, "What do you mean?"

"Look," I told him, "you don't need to protect your girlfriend from bullets—unless she's involved in organized crime or a drug cartel (in which case you need to make better dating decisions). You don't need to protect her from the mafia. You need to protect her from your lust. That's how you need to die for her."

This young man's desire to die for his beloved was a noble one. In fact, I believe that God has programmed within every man a desire to make a heroic sacrifice of himself for others. We want to storm the castle, kill the dragon, and save the princess. However, the problem with this fairy tale notion is that it always places the enemy outside of us; the beast that needs to be conquered is always an external foe. It's a humbling realization when we discover that the battlefield is inside our very hearts.

There's a war going on within every man between love and lust. One of the two will win, and to the victor will go the spoils: Whatever wins his heart (love or lust) will win his imagination, his eyes, his body, his vocation, and his very soul. Either the man will master his temptations for the sake of love, or his temptations will master him.

This may all sound over-dramatic, but let's be honest: Most of this war is unseen by the world. It's happening in a husband's conscience when he sees a pop-up ad on his laptop at night while his wife is asleep in another room. It's happening on a teen's cell phone when no one can see his screen. It's taking place in every guy's imagination and in his eyes every day.

Because the war is largely invisible to others, it's all too easy for guys who are being slaughtered on this battlefield to live as if they have everything under control. Many young men feel as if their chances for victory are slim. They've tried to break free from the vices of pornography and masturbation, but they feel like freedom is nowhere in sight.

For this reason, it's a surprise to me why a book such as the one you're holding wasn't written a long time ago. All I know is that it's overdue. In *Freedom*, Everett offers a concrete game plan for how to break free from habits of lust. In it, he doesn't propose a litany of coping mechanisms. Instead, based on his many years of experience of working with young men in ministry, he presents a practical, hopeful, and fully Catholic call-to-arms for how to find victory.

As you will learn through this book, purity is not about annihilating your desires or simply keeping them in check. In fact, the goal of this book isn't simply to convince you to trash pornography or to defeat habits of sexual sin. Rather, by rejecting lust, St. John Paul II explained that "we acquire the virtue of purity, and this means that we come to an ever greater awareness of the gratuitous beauty of the human body, of masculinity and femininity. This gratuitous beauty becomes a light for our actions."[1]

Did you catch that? So often, we think that the body *is* the problem. But St. John Paul is saying that as we battle for our purity, we'll discover the beauty of the body, and that this awareness of beauty will guide our actions. Therefore, the goal isn't to continually avoid the sight of what is beautiful, but to learn how to see the beauty of the human person with the eyes of God. In other words, the ultimate goal of purity is to be free to love. If there has ever been a war worth fighting, this is it.

Make no mistake, Everett's book is an invitation for you to come and die. But do not be afraid. As Jesus promised, "Truly, truly, I say to you, unless a grain of wheat falls into the earth and dies, it remains alone; but if it dies, it bears much fruit" (Jn 12:24).

Preface

The Reason for This Book

I have the honor of mentoring a small group of high-school boys who meet weekly to pray, study the Bible, and enjoy camaraderie. They also learn what it means to be Christian men, which is especially important in the present age, where the reaction to authentic Christianity and true manhood tends to run the gamut from sincere confusion to seething hostility. These two pillars of civilization tend to converge on issues of sexual morality that have come to define the battle lines in our culture wars: from abortion to homosexual "marriage," divorce to cohabitation, pornography to the gender-bending the media are bent on portraying as just another "lifestyle."

Once, one of the boys in our group wanted to talk about sexual morality during a typically freewheeling conversation. Basically, he wanted to know what it means to be chaste in this day and age, and if such-and-such behaviors were acceptable. (No, they weren't, but we'll get to that later.) It quickly became apparent that more than a quick conversation was needed to answer all the questions this boy raised, so I decided to discuss sexual purity with the group in a thorough, in-depth manner. So I went looking for a book to help guide our discussions over the coming weeks—one that could serve as a primer on sexual purity, which is indispensable to being a Christian man.

I was very specific in what I wanted this book to cover. In particular, I wanted a book that met three key criteria:

1. It had to address the topics of masturbation and pornography with the intention of mentoring young men through these issues and creating a detailed and specific action plan to guide them through the battle for purity.

2. God had to be engaged in this battle—disposing a person to receive God's grace and leading him to an encounter with Jesus Christ—because purity is impossible without God, the source of all purity.

3. The book had to be Catholic, specifically integrating the holistic and life-giving principles of Catholic moral teaching. Real purity is not about saying no to one's sexuality; it is about saying yes to God's plan and living in harmony with how he created us. Never have I seen this better articulated than in Catholic moral teaching.

I wasn't familiar with a book that met all three criteria, but I was sure that someone had to have written one because the need is so real. I contacted every major Catholic chastity speaker that I knew and asked where I could find a book integrating discipleship, sexual purity, and Catholic moral teaching for young men. To my great surprise, none knew of such a book. One of the speakers said that he had a small booklet for young men with a few pages devoted to the topic of masturbation. So I continued to ask others, thinking that someone must know about the kind of book I was looking for. To my surprise, no one did.

My search came up empty-handed. Yet this was not a cause for despair, but a challenging opportunity. I realized that I had something to offer on this particular subject. Conquering sexual impurity was a major turning point in my own life, and it had everything to do with transforming me into the man I have been blessed to become. I came to realize that my own journey and testimony might be helpful in mentoring teenage boys to become real men and help uplift a fallen culture.

With this book I hope to challenge you to become the man that you are created to be. I can help lead you to life-giving water but, like the proverbial horse, cannot force you to drink. Whether to become a man or stay forever a boy is, at bottom, up to you.

This book has three aims, which will bear fruit only with your cooperation:

1. To give you advice, encouragement, and a detailed plan to avoid or overcome sexual impurity.

2. To replace the tendency to objectify women with a full understanding of the relationship among love, sex, and manhood, thus inspiring you to live sexual purity with joy, happiness, freedom, and life-giving love.

3. To help you develop a close, genuine relationship with Jesus Christ, who is a real Person and the source of all that is pure and beautiful. I want you to know that Christ loves you beyond measure and wants to give you the grace and strength to live free from slavery to misguided passions—passions

that can lead to spiritual corruption and even the loss of your salvation.

Heaven is our intended destination, but it's not guaranteed. It all comes down to knowing the truth, living the truth, and exhilarating in the freedom that this alone can bring.

Introduction

Several years ago, I had a fourteen-year-old boy in my youth group named Joel. Joel was a good-looking, gregarious kid. Girls loved being around him, and other guys wanted to be like him. He was starting to come around the parish more often, and I was enjoying watching Joel on his search for manhood. As a youth minister, I had the privilege of being involved in the lives of many teens, and I got to know their lives and backgrounds very well. I have always found the mission of forming young people in the faith to be an inspiring and challenging calling. There are a lot of influences in the world that can lead a person away from Christ and his Church. As leader of the youth group, I intercept the lies that teenage boys often tell themselves and replace them with God's truth. When they accept truth in their lives, I witness them come alive and see their lives flourish. When the lies are not intercepted or the truth goes unembraced, the results can be disastrous.

Unfortunately for Joel, the latter proved true.

Joel had set a goal for himself to lose his virginity before his fifteenth birthday. His sister had lost hers at fifteen, and he wasn't going to be outdone. For Joel, it wasn't simply a struggle of hormones or relationships. *He had something to prove: to become a "man" through sexual conquest.* The goal wasn't unrealistic. After all, girls practically threw themselves at him. He set his sights on one, Mikala, a friend of his from childhood who always had seemed to take an interest in him. Mikala was a very pretty girl from a wealthy family. She had been going through some hard times recently, although Joel knew little about it. In Mikala he saw an attractive girl who was vulnerable and friendly, and he wanted to seize the opportunity. To be fair to Joel, his interest in Mikala wasn't purely physical—she was a good friend, and he had real personal interest in her. Joel asked Mikala to be his girlfriend. On their first date, they met up at their local country club. Before the day was through, they found an out-of-the-way place, and Joel achieved his goal.

Mission accomplished. Mikala had made a man *out of Joel.*

The story becomes even more sadly twisted. As their relationship progressed, Joel began to realize that Mikala was seriously troubled. She wanted to be with him all the time and would frequently become emotional when they were together. She was depressed and emotionally dependent. From a relationship standpoint, Joel had bitten off more than he could chew. While Joel enjoyed the sexual relationship, the other aspects of his relationship with Mikala were a lot more than he could handle. One night, Mikala dropped a bombshell on Joel. She had good reason to be a wreck: her father was in jail for child molestation.

Joel was in way over his head. Mikala would tell Joel that she was hurting, and many nights she would spend hours on the phone crying her heart out to him. She began having frequent panic attacks and told Joel that she wanted to commit suicide. Joel would try to be her support, but he knew he didn't have what it took to help her through her problems. Eventually, Joel ended the relationship, leaving Mikala when she was most in need. Mikala needed love, compassion, security, and an invitation to professional counseling. Joel could provide none of those things.

What Mikala needed was a MAN. What she got was a BOY.

The Difference Between Boys and Men

Joel and Mikala's story is sad, yet sadly commonplace nowadays. Joel's false understanding of what it means to be a real man is shared by many young men I have mentored over the years with varying degrees of success. Joel wanted to be a man, but he was very misguided in the actions that it takes to accomplish that noble goal. The end result was emotional pain and confusion, and definitely missing the mark on achieving manhood. So how does a boy become a man? What is the difference between boys and men?

I have three children, all currently under the age of six. Two of them are boys, so I see the difference between boys and men every day. As a husband and father, my life is devoted to my wife and children. From working to provide for them to helping my wife run the household, very little of my daily life is self-oriented. Rather, my efforts are directed toward serving the people that I love. My children, on the other hand, are basically focused on their own needs and wants: I WANT that toy, I WANT to watch TV, I WANT ice cream for dinner. It isn't until they get older that children begin to learn that the world does not—and even if it could, *should* not—revolve around them.

So how does a boy become a man? A boy grows into a man as he learns to put his strengths, gifts, and passions at the service of others. This should happen naturally as a boy grows older. However, I have noticed a troubling trend stifling such natural and wholesome growth, even preventing it from happening altogether: the modern-day scourge of immature boys inhabiting the bodies of adult males who shirk manly responsibilities from the adolescent security of their "man caves."

Two of the biggest obstacles preventing passage from boyhood to true manhood—not the false version epitomized by devotion to "beer, babes, and big-screen TVs"—are masturbation and pornography. It is no secret that many adolescent and adult males struggle with masturbation and pornography. They have become enslaved to the gratification of their own desires whenever they become aroused. Many justify this behavior because they do not think that masturbation or pornography "hurts" anyone. And after all, our culture tells males that their sexual desires need to be gratified, that practicing self-control isn't "natural," and repressing sexual desires might even cause psychological or physical damage.

But far from being healthy or liberating, masturbation and pornography enslave a man to his selfish desires. They are selfish because the intention of these practices is directed *entirely* to a person's own desires at the expense of another. Sexuality is designed by God to be shared with a person of the opposite sex in the context of exclusive, life-giving love. When a boy or adult male forms the habit of seeking his own gratification apart from a loving and committed relationship, he trains himself to treat members of the fairer sex as objects of pleasure instead of persons to be loved. Joel's story perfectly demonstrates this. Instead of helping Mikala, he took advantage of a vulnerable girl with a lot of baggage—a girl likely desperate for the fatherly guidance she couldn't find in her own child-molesting father—then discarded her after discovering his vehicle to "manhood" was broken and needed more support than he could give.

Seeking gratification through masturbation, pornography, and sexual promiscuity is void of love and, because it cannot satisfy the desires of the heart, leaves one feeling empty and unfulfilled. Even worse, it initiates a vicious cycle, tricking one into thinking that those deepest desires really will be satisfied if only one engages in the same behaviors ever more frequently and intensely. This is why "soft" pornography so often leads to ever "harder" displays of perversion. The result is the double woe of dissatisfaction and enslavement to one's passions. For adolescent boys, sexual impurity becomes a trap preventing them from becoming men because they never learn how to live for the good of another. Their impurity is a stumbling block to true love, which they confuse with lust.

Most men I know struggle with or have struggled with purity at one time or another. However, very few openly address their problem. This effectively means that sexual impurity is a deep, dark secret lurking in the heart of many a man too embarrassed to bring it out into the light. Allowed to fester in silence and grow in darkness, it can destroy relationships between the sexes—if those relationships are even allowed to form in the first place. Because of sexual impurity, many males never become the great men they are called to be, and many young women desiring to enter into unions of life-giving love are left waiting. Sadly, many women settle for imitations of manhood because they have given up hope that any real men actually exist. The resultant union of a boy and a woman—instead of a man and a woman—becomes a recipe for destruction and disaster in both of their lives, not to mention in the lives of any children they might have, especially boys who need their fathers to mentor them into manhood.

The challenge is clear: in order to fill the deficit of real men in the world, we need to address the problem of sexual impurity, which keeps boys, regardless of age, from becoming men and realizing their God-given potential.

Chapter 1

Where Are All the Real Men?

I was at an amusement park with my kids recently, where I observed a boy and a girl holding hands. They couldn't have been older than fifteen. The girl led the boy up to a carnival booth where the goal was to knock over a stack of bottles with a baseball. If you knocked over the bottles, you won a big stuffed teddy bear. I watched as the girl looked up at her boyfriend, smiled at him, and said, "Will you win me a prize?" The boy took out a five-dollar bill, handed it to her and replied, "You do it." That was not what the girl had in mind. She pleaded with him, but it was no use. The boy did not know what he was supposed to do, and he stood there looking at her—not understanding that there was a lot more to this simple interaction than throwing a baseball at some bottles. The girl ended up half-heartedly throwing the ball herself and leaving without a prize. She was disappointed, the boy was clueless, and I was dumbfounded. Someone needed to throw a ball at the boy's head. The girl had no interest in playing a silly carnival game or winning a big teddy bear. She wanted the boy to win her heart, but he was blind to the opportunity.

I contrasted this sad scene with another I witnessed at World Youth Day in Madrid in 2011. World Youth Day is a huge gathering of Catholic youth from around the world who meet every two to three years with the Pope and other leaders in the Church for a celebration of their Catholic faith. The event culminates with an all-night vigil followed by a huge outdoor Mass with the Pope the next morning. The event is incredible and many of the young people who attend credit it with producing major conversions.

During the all-night vigil in Madrid, after the Pope had finished the liturgical celebrations for the evening, I came across two Italians—a boy and a girl—in the crowd of some two million. It was hard to miss them. They were *all over each other*. This boy was the complete opposite of the boy at the carnival: *He knew exactly what he wanted to do and how to do it*. He knew where he was trying to lead this girl, and she seemed more than willing to go along. After a while I couldn't contain myself. I walked up behind the guy and; smacked him upside the head. Both turned and looked at me, and I was prepared to give him the best and most passionate chastity talk that I had ever given.

Then I realized I didn't speak Italian.

I settled for pointing my finger in his face and yelling, "NO!" At first they were startled, then they started laughing at me. All I could do was walk away in frustration. I realized that I might want to work on my Italian before ever pulling a stunt like that again.

Both of these examples reflect the same problem: So many young men are clueless when it comes to right relationships. In general, young men don't know how to love and lead a woman, unless they are trying to lead her to their own bedroom. When I speak to teenage girls, I tell them to keep their standards high—that a young man who courts them should be strong, chivalrous, and desire that they walk the path to heaven together. He should be pure in his intentions and unrelenting in valuing their common good over any selfish desires that could lead them both into sin. I tell young girls that these are the men that make great husbands and fathers and that they should hold out until they find a man who is willing to love them and lead them. Girls love this talk. It's exactly what they want to hear because they know in their hearts it's true. The problem is that many of the girls have called me out on it. They light up, full of hope and desire to be loved and cherished, and then they ask me the question, *"Where do I find a man like this? Where do I find a real man?"*

Umm…that's a great question.

I never have a satisfactory response.

Manhood in the Meatgrinder

For quite some time, we have been hearing about a vocations crisis in the Catholic Church, meaning a lack of men willing to commit to the priesthood. It is a theme that is often preached from the pulpit. The general idea is that the priests in the world are getting older and there are not enough young priests and seminarians in the ranks to replace the priests who are retiring and dying. The crisis is that one day there may be too few priests to meet the needs of the Catholic laity around the world. The Church has begun making an appeal for more men to step up and answer the call to the priesthood. I remember hearing one vocations director challenge a group of young men, saying, "We need *REAL MEN* to step up and become priests."

Why don't more Catholic men consider the priesthood? The requirements of celibacy and a life of service to the Church are certainly challenging. Perhaps men are being drawn to something else. After all, priesthood is not the only vocation open to men; marriage is another option. At first glance, one might think that all the real men are not considering a vocation to the priesthood because they want to have good, faithful, and holy marriages. So, are all the real men (and women) getting married and fully embracing that life-long vocation?

The following statistics paint a bleak picture:

- Around half of first-time marriages end in divorce, with the rate being even higher for subsequent re-marriages.[2]

- According to the U.S. Census Bureau, twenty-four million children in America—roughly one out of every three—live in homes without their biological father.[3]

- Nearly 30% of children living without their biological father haven't seen him in over a year, and over 20% see him only several times a year.[4]

- For several decades, around 20% of married men and 15% of married women admit to having had adulterous affairs, with the rate among younger couples having climbed in recent years.[5]

Add to this the fact that more people than ever are cohabiting without getting married, and illegitimate births are so common that they're accepted as normal, and it is clear that marriage is suffering a vocation crisis, too. The more that I reflect on the vocations crises in the Church, the more I am convinced that it is simply a symptom of a larger problem: There are not enough *real men* faithfully living out the vocation to marriage, and there are not enough *real men* answering the call to the priesthood because there are simply not enough *real men* in the world, period. Without priests, we have no Church. Without good husbands and fathers, the bedrock of civilization—strong marriages, families, and communities—is crumbling. In short, a healthy society requires real men. A sick society suffers a shortage of them.

The problem we face, however, is not simply a lack of good men.

It is that many people in our culture don't even know or understand what it means to be a man.

The Modern Message about Manhood

Have you ever noticed the enormous difference between Mother's Day cards and Father's Day cards? A Mother's Day card will express thanks and say something very wonderful about Mom. The general message is usually something like, "Our family could never live without you. Thank you for being such a wonderful mother. I love you." This sort of message is rarely communicated to dads when it comes to Father's Day cards.

A few days before Father's Day I went shopping for a card for my dad. I picked up three different cards. Here is what they said:

- Happy Father's Day...thanks for impregnating mom.

- Today, we honor you, dad...or as mom calls you, "the good for nothing."

- I wanted to give you something special on Father's Day...so I farted in this card.

Imagine that our civilization were one day destroyed, and hundreds of years later, people discovered several boxes of Father's Day and Mother's Day cards, labeled them as artifacts, and tried to decipher the values of our culture from them. What would they think about the roles of mothers and fathers in our culture? They would probably believe that mothers were the caring, nurturing, and compassionate parent, while fathers were good for nothing except procreating. And those dwellers in the distant future would not be far off the mark: Fathers are given far too little credit for their contributions to society, and popular culture rarely accords them the honor they deserve.

Take a look at modern sitcoms or comedies that involve a family. What role does the father play? He is almost always the butt of jokes. Men are portrayed as ignorant, incompetent, weak, and largely irrelevant, whereas women are depicted as the real heads of the house. In fact, it has been this way for decades. You would practically have to go all the way back to television series such as the Andy Griffith Show in the 1960s to find a strong father figure in a sitcom. In modern media, there are too few examples of real men who love, serve, and truly live out their vocations. Without a doubt, popular culture—that is, secular culture, which is not oriented toward God—does not give exemplars of manhood and, thus, does not encourage boys to become men.

Without an example of manhood in their lives, boys are forced to either learn about manhood from less than ideal sources or to discover it somehow on their own. The world is not presenting a real message about manhood. In fact, the bar for men is really quite low. Even worse, there are not enough men within the Church who are living witnesses of authentic manhood—and as a result, young men are not being mentored or inspired to greatness.

Why the Bad Examples?

St. John Paul II was once asked, "What is the biggest problem that you see in the world?" He could have replied, "famine, social justice, abortion," or any number of issues. Instead he said, "We do not have enough saints in the world."

But why?

Why aren't there more everyday saints giving living witnesses of manhood?

Why are so many men turning in on themselves instead of learning to serve others and the good of society?

What is enslaving them to a childish and self-centered mentality?

Why is this problem universal across the Western world?

My answer: *Sexual impurity.*

As I stated in the Introduction, sexual impurity has become widespread among the male population. When considering the universality of the crisis of manhood, we have to consider how this contributes to the crisis.

Consider the following statistics:

- In one poll, half of Christian men said they are "addicted" to pornography.[6]

- Nearly 68% of young adult men view pornography at least once a week.[7]

- Another poll found that 67% of young men (and, by the way, 49% of young women) think viewing pornography is an acceptable way to express one's sexuality, and 98% of college undergraduate males reported having masturbated.[8]

As these statistics show, the majority of young males regularly commit sins against purity. And this is preventing a large part of the population from becoming the men they were created to be, which goes a long way toward explaining the breakdown of the family and society.

If you are a male, and you are reading this book, there is a good chance that you fall into one of the statistics above. Yet, if you do struggle with sexual purity—even if you have developed a problem so habitual that you think you've lost the ability to break free from it—there is good news. There is a way to liberate yourself from enslavement to sin. There is a path to discovering your own masculinity in a way that you never knew was possible. You don't have to be a part of the problem… *You can be part of the solution.*

I know this to be the case from experience. I once was lost, but I found the way.

Chapter 2

My Story

If you have been reading up to this point, you may have figured out that I am a deeply religious person and try hard to be the man our Creator intended me to be. I haven't always been this way.

In my early teenage years, I was introduced to pornography. I encountered it for the first time when I was ten and discovered my uncle's stash of *Playboy* magazines. Then, when I was about thirteen, I actively started to look for pornography on the internet. It didn't take long for me to become hooked. I also was regularly masturbating by then. While I was brought up to understand that these practices were sinful and "dirty," I never had much conviction about their moral severity. After all, I didn't think I was hurting anyone. That I was hurting myself didn't dawn upon me until later.

While in high school, my dad changed jobs and our family relocated. Leaving old friends behind and trying to make new friends is not something that is particularly fun to do during one's adolescent years. The pain and loneliness that I experienced during that time drove me further into these sinful practices, as I sought comfort by turning inward on myself and my desire for love. Despite this period of loneliness, I met my first girlfriend at my new high school. Although we didn't have sex, our short-lived relationship was anything but pure.

I did not realize it at the time, but this period of self-indulgence in my life—the pornography, masturbation, and impure relationships—had begun warping my attitude toward women. I started thinking that women and their beauty existed for my pleasure and gratification and there was nothing wrong with reducing them to their bodies, then seducing them (or at least fantasizing about doing so). Like too many of my peers, I came to believe that sexual expression was to be experienced in continual conquests, certainly not a life-long relationship of love with one woman. This warped view led to a dangerous and destructive form of bondage over my life, which it nearly ruined. It also nearly ruined the lives of others, which exposes the lie that sexual impurity is OK because "it doesn't hurt anyone."

Sweet Sixteen: A New Love

When I was sixteen, I went on a Catholic youth retreat and began going to a youth group where I learned about God's love—a concept that had been lost on me up to that point. For the first time in my life, I was awakened to the idea of something greater than myself.

Attending the youth group was the best thing that could have happened to me. I started making friends, and the friendships we formed were rooted in a purpose and mission. While I was far from being a devout Catholic at that time in my life, these friendships were what kept me coming back to meetings.

In that youth group, I started to get to know a girl who would change my life forever. Her name was Katrina, and she attended my high school. Katrina was the most beautiful girl I had ever seen—she was way out of my league—and over the course of several months, we became very close friends. I had never had a friend like her: I really cared about what was best for her. In spite of the fact that I had a big-time crush on her, Katrina made it really clear up-front that she did not have any interest in a romantic relationship with me. Friendship is what she wanted, and, in spite of my feelings for her, I was happy to oblige.

As I got to know her, and as we learned more about each other, Katrina began to share with me that she had a serious struggle in her life. She liked to "party." And she partied a lot. It wasn't until she went on a Church retreat—the same one that I had been on—that her eyes were opened and she realized that her drinking and partying had led her into a seriously destructive lifestyle. At the age of fifteen, Katrina had spent the better part of the summer drunk and began finding it hard to imagine life without a drink in her hand. On the retreat, she realized that God wanted her to stop this sinful behavior. But most of her friendships were based around partying, and she was struggling to give it up. I had become the one friend in her life who wasn't part of that scene—whose idea of a good time wasn't getting wasted—and she needed my friendship to help her break free. Little did I know how much her friendship would help me.

The Night that Changed My Life

One night, while talking on the phone, she told me about something bad that had happened to her several months earlier at a party. There was an older boy who had an agenda. She had caught his eye, and he kept trying to put drinks in her hand. She tried to keep her distance, but by the end of the night, she narrowly escaped rape.

When she told me the story, I was *infuriated*.

I didn't know the boy, so I couldn't vent my anger by taking him to task. Instead, after I got off the phone, I went down to my basement to lift weights and pump out my aggression.

That is when I heard God speak to me for the first time in my life.

I'd like to say that he said something really loving or encouraging. That was not the case.

God said to me, "*Why are you angry at this boy? You are no different.*"

I was shocked and horrified at this. I responded, "I would *NEVER* do that! I would never force myself on a girl—certainly never on my friend!"

God responded, "*You do it when you look at pornography; you do it when you fantasize and masturbate; and you would do it with Katrina if she gave you the opportunity. You might not take her by force, but take her you would.*"

I stood there in my basement, completely stunned. I had been convicted by God, who knows all and sees all, *and I was guilty.* The intentions of my heart were no different from that other boy's. I was a user of women. I could not stand the thought of having the same impure intentions as the guy who tried taking Katrina by force—the guy I wanted to level! In that moment, I realized how horribly sinful my attitude toward women had become, and how my attachments to impure thought and action could wreak havoc upon me and any woman I tried getting close to. I stood alone in my basement… and I wept.

I knew that I was not the man that I wanted to be and that something was deeply wrong with the intentions of my heart and the actions of my body. Something needed to change and it needed to happen now.

My Journey to Freedom

I wanted to change my life. For the sake of my friend and for the sake of all women I wanted to be a good man, not a weak boy. I may have been helpless to defend Katrina from that guy at the party, but I was not helpless to defend her from myself. I determined to stop looking at pornography and to stop masturbating. I wanted to be pure for my future bride. I wanted to be pure of heart. I wanted to be a real man.

I never realized how difficult it would be. Within a few days of making this commitment so earnestly, I had already broken it. I hadn't given up, but I was less free than I had ever realized. The sin was firmly entrenched in my thought process and daily habits, and it was not surrendering without a fight. At the early age of seventeen, I realized something about my life that frightened me: I was a virtual slave to sins from which I desperately wanted to be free.

Alcoholics Anonymous is famous for the twelve-step program that provides a path to freedom from addiction. Those who go through the program must work through those twelve steps in their lives so that they can one day say that their substance addiction no longer controls them. The first step is admitting that they have a problem. The second is admitting that there is a higher power that is greater than them. And the third is making a decision to turn over their will to the care of God.

But I hadn't reached the third step yet, and was trying to break free from sin through my own power alone. After each fall into sexual impurity, I would re-commit myself to being chaste. Time and again I would fall, and time and again I would re-commit. It helped immensely to have my friendship with Katrina, who kept me motivated with her support. But after several months of trying, I still could not kick these sinful habits. Something was missing. I lacked a weapon to win my battle against impurity.

One night after giving up the fight and succumbing to self-gratification, I finally fell into despair. I wanted to quit but didn't think I could stop. It was then that I turned to Jesus. I prayed for his help and his mercy. I prayed for him to pick me up and carry me. I knew that I could not be a free man on my own. I needed Jesus to help me. In one word, I *surrendered*.

Christ's response was simple: *"Come, follow me."*

From that moment, the fight was different. Every time I felt like giving up the battle, he found a way to hold me accountable and support me. When I prayed, I was encouraged. When I fell, there was Christ's mercy available in the Sacraments, especially the Sacrament of Reconciliation. There was a time when once again I felt like giving up entirely, but prayed for God to send me some support. The next day, our high school had an unannounced chastity presentation that gave me the exact encouragement I needed. Christ was there for me. I followed him and he led me to freedom.

Freedom in Christ

After several months without falling, I can remember the moment when I finally realized that I was free. I no longer had a desire to use women for my own gratification, and pornography and masturbation no longer had dominion over me. I had found a strength and security that I never realized was possible. I had discovered the liberating power of disciplines in my life and principles to live by. The experience of freedom was overwhelming and amazing.

I said to Jesus, "If this is the way that you bless me when I surrender one area of my life to you, then I want to surrender *everything* to you." I prayed that Christ would take everything in my life and lead me to be his disciple. I had discovered a relationship with Jesus Christ through the virtue of chastity and I now wanted to serve Christ with my entire life. I can look back on that prayer now, many years later, and marvel at the abundant blessings in my life. Jesus promised us that, "I came that they might have life, and have it abundantly" (Jn 10:10), and this promise becomes reality when we give everything to him.

Shortly after I made this commitment to Christ, Katrina confessed to me that she had developed very serious feelings for me. She had also made a commitment to Christ and had walked away from her destructive lifestyle. We had supported each other in virtue and led each other to Christ. Now Christ was blessing our relationship with a newfound love.

We started dating in our senior year of high school, and we dated all the way through college. The strength and discipline that I had found in my journey to freedom became essential as we grew into adulthood and our love matured. We supported each other through hardships, healing, and into a holy relationship. Three weeks after we graduated from college, we were united together in Holy Matrimony, starting a new life together as "one flesh." God blessed our love, our commitment to him, and our commitment to purity—and he continues to bless us today. We exercised the virtue of chastity before and after marriage, chastity being the sexual expression appropriate to one's state in life. Chastity means no sexual relations before you're married, and if married, only with your spouse in a complete self-giving that's open to new life. Without chastity and without Jesus Christ, there is no way that our marriage or our children's lives would ever have come into being.

My Story and Yours

My testimony and the decisions I have made in my life have allowed me to see life from two radically different perspectives: slavery to sexual sin and freedom in Christ through holy living. I can tell you that I would much rather be free than enslaved to sexual desires, which ensnare many a man by giving an illusory sense of freedom. I learned that when we use women, instead of valuing them as persons to be protected and cherished, we hurt them, and we hurt ourselves.

So, what about you? Are you a "user" or do you cherish and love women? When it comes to the desires of your flesh, are you a real man? Do you seek to serve the people you love, or are you only focused on yourself? Take the following quiz. No pencils are necessary. Just be honest with yourself and answer yes or no to the following questions:

1. Do you deliberately fantasize about sex?

2. Do you undress women in your mind?

3. Do you allow your eyes to gravitate to certain features of women's bodies?

4. Do you seek out relationships with women just so you might satisfy your lust?

5. Do you speak about women as sexual objects when you are with other guys?

6. Do you watch movies because they have sexually explicit scenes?

7. Do you view pornography?

8. Do you have pornography saved on your computer, mobile device, or hidden in another secret place?

9. Do you masturbate?

10. Are you single and sexually active? (Sexually active involves contact with any private places on the body.)

If you answered yes to any of these questions, then you are using women for your own gratification. (If a woman is willing to be used, and wants to use you in return, that is no justification for immorality, either.) The world needs real men, who are pure and will take the challenge to stand up and love women in truth and virtue. Sexual sin is a problem that most men face, and temptation abounds in a culture so hyper-sexualized that even young girls feel compelled to dress seductively as a means to draw attention to themselves. If you are willing to stand up and take a stand for the dignity of manhood, then God will bless your desire for purity. The journey to freedom begins with changing our understanding of our own sexuality and sexual expressions. As I learned, there is an enormous difference between the messages that the world tells us about sex and God's plan for human sexuality.

Chapter 3

The Promise of Sex

Have you ever been in line at a grocery store and seen the front covers of some of the magazines? It's hard not to, and that's the point. *Cosmopolitan* stands out to me the most because it always has cover stories that are variations on "101 Great Sex Moves that Will Blow His Mind!" or "The Hot Sex Move that Every Guy Wishes You Knew!" or "42 Sex Secrets for Your Hottest Sex Ever!" People must be buying this magazine because it has been around forever. When I was a teenager, I let my curiosity get the better of me and picked up a copy. I realized it was a mistake as soon as I started reading the sex tips. Several of the tips were cliché and really stupid, but the one that really caught my eye was "Use a blow dryer on each other. You are sure to feel a rush every time you feel the heat!" I read that tip and thought to myself, "Are you crazy?! Who in his right mind wants to be burned with a blow dryer while making love?!"

But that is exactly the problem. When it comes to sex, people are not in their right minds. Sex is an incredible experience, but when it is taken out of the context for which it was created, it leaves a person feeling like it is insufficient. The fact that *Cosmopolitan* has been able to survive for so long while giving different sex tips every month reflects how unsatisfied people are with their sex lives. But it also raises the question, "What makes for good sex?"

The World's Confusion about Sex

I attended a Catholic high school that used to host a yearly presentation on abstinence. It usually consisted of someone telling us why we shouldn't have sex and trying to scare us into chastity. Needless to say, the student body didn't react well to this tactic. After one of these presentations, I remember getting into the lunch line and overhearing my classmate say, "What a stupid presentation! Why should I wait to have sex until I'm married? I'm pretty sure my wife would want me to know what I am doing before I get married." This is the type of comment I have heard several times, but it is faulty logic.

So, let's say you are a virgin, and you are engaged to be married. You don't want to be inexperienced on your wedding night, so you decide to hire a prostitute one week before the wedding so that you can get in some practice. If your wife finds out about this, is she going to say, "Thank goodness you got in some practice before the wedding! I was worried that you wouldn't know what to do." Any virtuous woman would be disconcerted, to put it mildly, about the kind of man she married.

About ten years ago, I was channel surfing and discovered a "reality" TV show called *Chaotic*. It was a short-lived series about the courtship, dating, and marriage of Britney Spears and Kevin Federline. Britney Spears was the sex icon of the era, and her sexual exploits were regularly captured in her music and personal image and then plastered upon the public eye. I didn't watch the show for very long (it was almost unwatchable, which explains why it was canceled after five episodes), but Britney said something at one point that really caught my attention. Kevin asked her, "What makes sex really good?" She thought about it for a second and responded, "I think it's good when you are *really into the person.*" In terms of sexual practice, she is someone who had supposedly done it all. Yet, she discovered that the most meaningful sexual intimacy goes beyond the physical act. Rather, it involves a deep connection between two people. It might come as a shock to Britney, but she was not that far off from what God and the Church teach us about sex: that to be good, it must be bound up in love.

God's Plan for Love and Sex

When many people think of what the Church has to say about sex, they see a big sign flashing "NO!" That is a fair opinion when you consider that this is the message most people have heard from people representing the Church:

- NO sex before marriage!

- NO kissing, touching, or intimacy of any sort!

- NO masturbation!

- NO pornography!

- If you do any of these things, you will get pregnant or get STDs and bad things will happen to you!

- You will go to hell if you break the rules!

Of course, this is not a fair representation of Church teaching, but it tends to be the impression of many people who haven't read the *Catechism of the Catholic Church*. It is easy to see why so many people are uninspired by a message emphasizing the negative. It just seems like a bunch of bad news around the topic of sex. The fullness of the Church's teaching on sexuality is not so much a "no" to its abuses, but a resounding "yes" to the fundamental goodness of this God-given gift.

According to the Church there are two purposes for sexual expression in marriage. The first is pretty self-evident: its procreative purpose. Sexual relations can lead to new human life. Since the rearing of a child is a lifelong commitment, it makes sense that sexual relations should only occur after the lifelong commitment of marriage has been made.

Furthering the human race is a necessary purpose of sexual relations. However, it would be inaccurate to claim that it is the only purpose. All animals instinctually copulate to further their own species, and tend to do so only at specific times when they are "in heat." However, generally, the union between the two animals ends when that purpose is achieved. Even for animals that stay together to protect and care for their young, the connection between the mates is far different from that of human beings. A goose couple doesn't choose to stay together, but does so by instinct.

We are different from other animals because we are spiritual beings with immortal souls. Made in the image and likeness of God, we have an intellect, a free will, and the ability to make rational choices. Because we can rise above instinct and make free choices, we have the ability to love. Love may elicit all sorts of feelings, but love itself is more than a feeling. Feelings are fleeting and the infatuation stage of a romance tends to serve as a sort of booster rocket that may launch a relationship of love into orbit, but burns out over time. Love is fundamentally an act of the will: choosing to "will the good of another," even when you might not feel all that lovey-dovey toward her.

According to the Church, sexual relations have a second purpose for spouses: to cultivate mutual love. Sexual expression is unitive in nature. It is intended to bring spouses closer together. In marriage, a man and a woman commit to love each other in good times and bad, in sickness and health, and until death does them part. When the two vow to give their entire lives to one another, the giving of their bodies to one another makes sense. Sexual relations between a husband and wife support and communicate marital love.

Language of the Body

That sexual relations are important in the relationship between a man and a woman should be no surprise. The body speaks a language of its own. If I wave to someone, he knows I mean to say hello. If I punch a person in the face, he knows that I am angry and want to fight. You cannot change the language of the body—I could never punch a person and tell him that I only meant to say hello. The action of a punch in the face has an unmistakable meaning.

Sexual relations are a language of the body as well— and one would imagine they have a powerful meaning. If the language of punching someone in the face communicates an undeniable and powerful message, how much more powerful and undeniable is the message of sexual relations? But what exactly is that message?

We have to go back to the beginning to understand the meaning of sexual relations. God is the author of sexual relations. In Genesis, when speaking of Adam and Eve, the Bible tells us that the two "become one flesh" (Gn 2:24). This is what God intended for Adam and Eve, and it was pleasing to him. In fact, the first commandment that God ever gave to mankind was, "Be fruitful and multiply" (Gn 1:28). How would mankind do this? They would procreate through sexual relations.

While all animals reproduce, only human beings *procreate*, because only we can collaborate with God in the creation of new beings made in his divine image and likeness. While the parents contribute the physical matter for the procreation of a new human being, God infuses an immortal soul. When a man and woman are united in the act of sexual relations and become "one flesh," they have the capability of procreating (that is "creating with" God) a new person. In short, starting with our first parents, God created marriage and blessed the sexual relations between a husband and a wife.

Sexual relations bring a man and woman together in love—closer, in fact, to God. Remember, "God is love" (1 Jn 4:8). It unites them, communicates love between them, and has the possibility of procreating a child who can then be reared within the love between them. In sexual relations, love is always the goal, and the language that the body speaks is love.

But that raises a question: What *kind* of love should sexual relations express? For there are many kinds of love. Unfortunately, English-speakers have only word for love, whereas other languages, like Greek, have several words that differentiate the different kinds of love. One word for love leads to a lot of confusion.

Love, Sex, and Marriage

My friend Mary Beth Bonacci, a well-known speaker and author on the subject of chastity, demonstrates this by talking about pizza. I love pizza, but that type of love would not be the same type of love that I communicate with my wife. If I don't finish my pizza, I put it in the fridge. If the pizza stays in the fridge too long and it is no longer appetizing, I throw it away. If I treated my wife the same way that I treated pizza, then we would have some serious marital problems. In fact, if I treated anyone the same way I treated pizza, then that wouldn't be love at all. It would be using the person to fulfill my own selfish appetites. There is a philosophical term for this called *utilitarianism*.

Remember that love requires *willing the good of the other*. Love between any two people—husband and wife, father and son, best friends at school—demands selflessness and sacrifice, compromise and lots of compassion. For example, I love my children, but there was one time when my son came into our bedroom at three in the morning because he was sick, then vomited in our bed. I did not harbor warm feelings for him at that moment. However, I did what was good for him. I got out of bed, comforted him in his illness, gave him a bath, got him some medicine to make him feel better, put him back to bed, and then changed the sheets in my own room. I did not throw him out like stale pizza and let him take care of himself. I love my son, and love required me to disregard my own comfort—I get too little sleep as it is—and do what was best for him.

If sexual relations speak a language of love, then it would make sense that the love communicated in sexual relations is about more than just physical pleasure. There must be a deeper message communicated in the sexual relations between a man and a woman.

Like all languages, the "language" of sexual relations has rules, which in this case were written by the Divine Author himself. What are the rules for properly expressing sexual relations?

- Sexual relations are designed to be *freely given*. God does not desire for anyone to be forced into a sexual relationship. Both man and woman should come together of their own free will, without external or internal coercion.

- Sexual relations are designed to be *total*, entailing a *complete gift of self*. In the act of sexual relations the man and woman give their entire bodies and persons to one another. They hold nothing back. They present a total self-gift of love.

- Sexual relations are designed to be *faithful*. The language of sexual relations says, "I give myself to *you* and no one else."

- Sexual relations are designed to be *fruitful*, uniting the couple in a deep bond of love that is open to the procreation of new life.

So why is it so important to understand God's plan for sexual relations and what he wants communicated by it? The language of freely given, total, faithful, and fruitful love is expressed in the promises and vows that two Christians make in the Sacrament of Matrimony. When my wife and I were married, we made three essential promises: we freely consented to enter marriage; we acknowledged marriage as an indissoluble union of mutual love and respect; and we were prepared to welcome children and bring them up in the Catholic faith. Then we exchanged vows that we would be faithful to one another in good times and in bad, in sickness and in health, until death do us part.

These were our promises and vows. Only after we had made these promises to God and to each other were we ready to express fully these vows with our bodies. An analogy of that love is found in the Bible in the relationship between Christ and his Church.

The Bridegroom and Bride

Do you know one of the terms used to describe Christ in the Bible? He is often referred to as the bridegroom and the Church as his bride. In the Book of Revelation, St. John's vision ends with a triumphant Christ united with his spotless bride (the Church) in heaven. The Bible begins with God creating Adam and Eve in a state of marriage so they can be co-creators with him, and it culminates in the "marriage" between Christ and his Church. In fact, the Bible can be described as one big love story between God and mankind.

But how does Christ fulfill the role of bridegroom? What is the significance of this title? Think about sexual relations. In the union of man and woman, the man gives himself to the woman so they can procreate new life. This is a reflection of the way that God interacts with his people. He pursues his people and through the grace of Baptism gives himself and his divine life: they become God's adopted sons and daughters. As such, when a husband has sexual relations with his wife, he isn't just communicating *his* love and *his* vows to his wife. He is also communicating and imaging *Christ's love for his bride, the Church*. Sexual relations between a husband and a wife, when entered into with freedom and total self-giving, are not just about love but also about worshipping God and imaging his love to each other and to the world. Thus are husband and wife intended to mirror the love between the divine bridegroom and his mystical bride, the Church. While all analogies of God's love are inadequate, the image of Christ and his Church as the bridegroom and bride is the least inadequate analogy. How powerfully is marriage therefore meant to reflect God's love!

God's Plan vs. The World's Idea

Let's take another look at God's plan for our sexuality as it relates to manhood. To be pure and true, sexual relations require love—not just any love, but a life-long commitment of love. This involves sacrifice, commitment, a mission, a bride, and not just a communion with that bride alone, but with God himself. Sexual relations remind us where we have come from (the union between Adam and Eve), tell our mission in the present (the union with our spouse within marriage), and give a foretaste of the eternal destiny to which we are called (complete and everlasting union with God in heaven). Seen in this light, sexual relations are a wondrous gift: selfless, meaningful, fulfilling, and sanctifying.

Now let's take another look at the world's plan for our sexuality as it relates to manhood. It involves no permanent commitment and seeks self-gratification and pleasure as the highest goals. In the case of masturbation and pornography, there isn't even a real person with whom we can communicate love. It turns our expression of sexuality entirely inward and our interest becomes concerned only with "fulfilling" our appetites and desires. Even in the context of a dating relationship between two people who may love each other, sex does not communicate true love, which requires a life-long, exclusive vow of commitment. Rather than expressing truth, sex between two such people is acting out a lie. By its very nature a lie cannot give genuine satisfaction. So I was not surprised when I read the finding of a Family Research Council study on which demographic of people have the most satisfying sex lives: devout Catholic married couples.[9] Not only did they have more fulfilling sexual relations, they were intimate more often!

Remember that example of *Cosmopolitan* magazine at the beginning of the chapter: *101 Sex Secrets to Change Your Life, etc., ad nauseum*? The fact that some people seriously read these magazines, earnestly searching for kinky tips to improve their sex lives suggests there's a lot of dissatisfaction out there. There is something within many a heart that is not being fulfilled, and so there are people who seek fulfillment by trying to gratify themselves through all manner of sexual immorality. But void of real love, no form of sexual arousal can fulfill our deepest desires.

I believe that it is this yearning for deeper meaning and intimacy that explains why so many males are drawn to pornography and masturbation. They are indeed "hollow men," desperate for fulfillment. But they seek fulfillment in the very things that drain them of their masculinity. Without knowing and living the purpose and meaning for sex, men are doomed to fall for the cheapest imitation. And so they engage in sexual impurity. Now that we know the problem, let me introduce you to the solution.

Chapter 4

"Come, Follow Me"

There is a strange phenomenon in our culture where the elderly and weathered have been labeled as "old" and "obsolete." We are one of the few cultures in the history of civilization that does not value the elderly for their wisdom. You would think that people would want advice from those who have been through all of the struggles and trials of this life in order to avoid becoming damaged physically and spiritually, perhaps irreparably. But many people seem to take pride in learning everything for themselves the hard way.

This applies to love, sex, and all manner of relationships. I once heard a young man challenge an article that I had written on relationships, saying that he knew more about women than I did because he had dated seventeen different girls over the past year. Being in a lot of failed relationships is more of an indictment than a badge of honor! From whom would you rather receive marriage advice, a person who has been divorced five times or a person who has been married for fifty years? When you are traveling to a place you have never visited before, would you rather get directions from someone who has been there already or someone who has gotten lost many times trying to get there and has yet to succeed?

Becoming a pure person can seem like a difficult journey. It's understandable to be afraid of getting lost along the way. But God never expects us to make any such journey on our own. *He wants to lead us along the way.*

And yet, despite whatever apprehension we might have about the difficulty of the journey or of getting lost, pride sometimes can prove overpowering. We can be tempted into being that fictitious American hero, the "rugged individual" who supposedly needs no one, not even God. We might foolishly set out to climb dangerous mountains all by ourselves just so that when (or if) we reach the top, we can say, "I did that on my own!" But this is not wise, and it is not the way that God intended us to live our lives. Jesus invited us to be his disciples, literally, learners. This requires humility, which is precisely what Satan lacked when he wanted to follow himself instead of God. And look where that got him.

Christ's Invitation

It's a big deal to be a disciple. Back in Jesus's day, only the most elite students would be allowed to be the disciple of a rabbi, which means teacher. A Jewish boy would start studying the Torah (the first five books of the Old Testament) when he was three. If he proved to be an excellent student, he would be invited to go to the next school, and then the next after that, until only the brightest students remained. At the end of the formal schooling, a rabbi would approach each boy and either invite him to become his disciple or tell him, "Go and learn the trade of your father." Only the best of the best were invited to study with a rabbi.

When a boy became a rabbi's disciple, he lived with his teacher. His education wasn't limited to simply the teachings and lessons of the rabbi. He learned from the rabbi's daily example—the way that he approached life and related to people. An old saying was that the disciple would be "covered in the dust of the rabbi" because he would follow the rabbi so closely that he would be covered in the dust kicked up from the rabbi's sandals.

Jesus invited grown men to be his disciples—men who, because they were practicing trades (e.g., fishing and collecting taxes), evidently had not been considered worthy to study under a rabbi and become teachers of the Law. Now they were given the opportunity to learn under the greatest rabbi ever, God himself, though they did not know this at first. He extended to them a simple invitation: "Follow me" (Mt 4:19). For the first disciples—the Twelve Apostles—they were getting a second chance. They may not have been the "best" students, but Jesus saw in them the potential for a kind of greatness surpassing mere intellectual brilliance. In faith and trust these men left everything behind to follow Jesus and become not just his disciples, but his friends. With the exception of Judas, all would die "covered in the dust" of their Teacher.

Our Need to Be Led

After Christ died and rose from the dead, the twelve Apostles—Matthias was selected to replace the original twelfth, Judas—became the leaders of the early Church. The Apostles went out into the world and lived among the people. They founded Christian communities and led the greatest revolution the world has ever seen. Christianity spread like wildfire, ignited by hearts on fire with the Good News of salvation through Jesus Christ. The Apostles were great leaders precisely because they had learned how to follow. Jesus never said to the Apostles, "Come, lead me." He said to them, "Follow me."

The Apostles learned from Jesus by his daily example. They watched and learned from everything that he did—the way he loved, prayed, handled adversity, related to people, enjoyed relaxation, and so forth. They learned from God himself, and, because they followed in his footsteps, the Apostles became the great men that they were created to be. They were no longer ordinary men, but saints, meaning holy ones, entrusted with carrying on the work of Christ in the world.

When we speak of journeying from impurity to loving and living God's amazing plan for our sexuality, there are steps that need to be taken. There are two options for taking the journey: going it alone or following the lead of another. When we choose to walk the path alone, we rely on our own strength. We have to learn from our own mistakes, and we have to be our own guides. Because of this, the chances of reaching our destination, at least without undue hardship, are slim. But when we follow the path with Jesus leading the way, the Holy Spirit gives us the strength to carry on, Jesus picks us up when we fall, and he reassures us of the rightness of our journey if we ever have doubts or get discouraged and want to return to the predictable misery of our unhappy home. Trusting in Jesus as our guide and following his lead, we cannot fail to arrive at our true home—a shelter impenetrable against the wickedest storm because it's constructed out of the goodness, truth, and beauty whose source is God himself.

We Need a Savior

To be a Christian means to acknowledge something every man and woman knows deep down: that we need help. In short, we need a savior. When we surrender our lives to Christ and allow him to rescue us from bondage to sin, we learn to rely on the grace the Holy Spirit bestows upon us. Grace is God's very life working within us. As the *Catechism of the Catholic Church* states, "Grace is *favor*, the free and undeserved help that God gives us to respond to his call to become children of God" (*CCC* 1996). Grace is a supernatural aid that helps us to be virtuous and follow God. When we learn to follow him, we learn to rely on his grace. When we receive the Sacraments, when we pray for God's grace, and when we follow Jesus day-by-day, we rely on his grace. The grace of God changes us from the inside out. And the hardest work of converting our hearts and minds is done by God himself. Grace, in short, is an awesome gift that no man can give himself.

When you have used your sexuality for your own selfish gratification and turned in on yourself, especially if you lived such a way for a long time, the journey to freedom can be exceedingly difficult. Jesus understands this, which is why he never intended for us to walk that journey alone.

Disciplines of a Disciple

The word disciple comes from the Latin root word *discere*, meaning to learn. Another word that shares the same root is *discipline*. Disciples learn to be disciplined persons in their everyday lives. They follow the rabbi's example, day-by-day, step-by-step, until they become like the rabbi.

In the same way, moving from impurity to purity in your life requires learning to be disciplined and to practice good habits. Jesus does the work internally as you learn to practice daily disciplines that open you more and more to God's grace. Your salvation—your freedom from sexual impurity—is a joint effort. It requires cooperating with the work of Christ in your heart and mind and being receptive to God's grace. Sinning is saying no to God and the transformative power of his grace. Because we have free will, God allows us to reject his grace. But that same free will was designed so that we might accept his grace.

This book's intention is to introduce you to Christ and to give you a battle plan of daily disciplines and habits that will help free you from impurity—or, if you are free from such bondage, to strengthen you in purity and help you grow more in your masculinity. For the next several chapters, we will examine the chains that bind men to sexual impurity. We will discuss how to develop habits of virtue and daily disciplines to break these chains. The disciplines you learn to practice will replace bad habits with good ones. Through these battle strategies, you will gradually renew your mind and heart in love. Christ will lead you to freedom. I pray this book will guide you in following his lead.

The First Discipline: Prayer

The most important discipline to learn is to pray—and to pray well. When we are children we are taught recited prayers, or simple prayers, so that we learn to develop the habit of prayer. Unfortunately, many people never grow past these initial introductions to prayer. Prayer is about encountering and communicating with a Person. In order to become free from impurity, we need to follow Christ, and this is impossible without talking to him. Jesus died and *rose from the dead*—He is alive. When we learn to pray well, we can find strength, grace, comfort, intimacy, and answers in the living Christ. Learning to pray well takes time, but Jesus guides us if we remain steadfast in our determination to know, love, and serve him.

To win the battle for sexual purity, you will need to learn to pray, and you need to do it every day. Daily prayer is a necessary discipline of any disciple of Jesus Christ. Jesus prayed constantly and with great intensity. And as the Master prayed, so must his disciples.

Learning to pray is simple, if you allow Christ to guide you. Here are four basic steps:

1. Begin with a moment of silence to find some internal peace and recollection.

2. Imagine Christ in front of you. Become aware of his presence. This will help you articulate your prayer to a Person, instead of feeling like you are talking into thin air.

3. Ask for the help to pray well, since we "don't know how to pray as we ought" (Rom 8:26), and then express your desires, sorrows, thanksgivings, and

praise to God. This can be a memorized prayer, if you can't think of anything to say.

4. Express contrition for any sins you've committed, and if they are serious or mortal sins, promise to go to the Sacrament of Reconciliation as soon as possible.

Your prayers don't need to be long, but pray you must. The journey to freedom, to being a man of Christ in full, begins with the first step of following Jesus's example and learning to pray. All other disciplines that are suggested in future chapters will not work unless you commit to this first discipline.

Beginning the Journey

As we have seen, our world needs real men—men who are capable of true love. Our world needs men who will follow Jesus and who are free from selfish, childish desires. Many women are waiting and looking for such men. Children need men like these to help them become mature and loving adults themselves one day. Our society is dying for lack of good men. Heaven is calling you to be one of them.

Will you answer the call?

Will you take the high road to strength and fulfillment or be content to slide down the slippery slope of weakness and inner desolation?

Have no false expectations: The journey to freedom will be difficult. But the first step is not. The first step is giving Jesus permission to lead you. If you are willing to begin the journey, then pray the following prayer:

Lord Jesus Christ, I pray that you would take me by the hand and lead me to freedom from sexual impurity. I pray that I may know you intimately, that you would reveal yourself in my life. I pray that I may know you better and grow closer to you every day. Jesus, I know that the journey will be difficult, and I ask that you will strengthen me for it. Jesus, I pray that you will bring to light my wounds that are attached to sexual impurity and that you will bring healing to those wounds. I pray that you will bring relationships into my life that will support my commitment to chastity. I ask you to remove relationships that pull me away from you. I pray that you will guide me through temptation and protect me from evil and selfishness. Jesus, be my teacher. Teach me to love. Teach me to pray. Teach me to be like you—to be the man that you created me to be. Should I struggle, carry me through that struggle. Should I fall, have mercy on me and lead me back to you and to your Sacraments. Guide my intentions, desires, and actions to purity and chastity. Help me, Lord, to never give up the fight and to be able to declare—for the glory of God—that I am free from any attachment to these sins. I ask this in the name of the Father, and of the Son, and of the Holy Spirit. Amen.

Thank you for committing to undertake this journey. The road ahead can seem difficult; the task of traveling it may appear daunting, even impossible. That is why it is so important to stay focused on the task for today. Committing to chastity for a lifetime can seem like an unachievable goal. But committing to it for today is something that you can accomplish. A wise woman once told me that "living in the future is living in a graceless moment." This means that God is present, as is his grace, here and now in this very moment. Thinking about tomorrow only brings anxiety and worry. As the great Mother Teresa of Calcutta said, "Yesterday is gone, tomorrow has not yet come. We have only today. Let us begin."

Chapter 5

The Root of the Problem

Have you ever seen the commercials in which a big, tough-looking truck is being driven through some rugged terrain like the Grand Canyon as a deep, manly voice says something like:

- "More horsepower than any other truck."

- "Strong, like a rock."

- "Built Ford tough."

You won't hear the commercial carefully explain all the features that make this truck better than any other on the market. These commercials aren't meant to appeal to your reason but to your emotions. After all, chances are you never are going to drive a pick-up in the Grand Canyon, haul around horses, go off-roading in the desert, or do any of the other *manly* things that truck commercials portray. Chances are you don't even need a big, bad pick-up, especially if you live in the suburbs and wear a white collar to work. These appeals to our emotions are meant to override our reason.

Truck commercials aren't the only ones that often appeal to sentiment over good sense. The marketing of many major products for men—from electronics, to deodorants, to beer—aims at eliciting an emotional response. You *need* this product right now because it will make your life better. *You will be a man. Women will want you.*

Marketers understand a key principle of the human person: *If you can generate an emotional response, you can influence behavior.*

This is one of the most important things to understand when it comes to sexual impurity, which, like so much of advertising, really boils down to internalizing lies.

Intellect, Will, Emotions, and Passions

St. Augustine broke down the human person into four parts: the intellect, the will, the emotions, and the passions. Your passions are your appetites, the things that tell you to eat, sleep, and engage in sexual activity. Your emotions are your feelings toward something. Your intellect is your faculty of reason. And your will allows you to make decisions.

Let me demonstrate how this works. Let's say you see a doughnut sitting on a plate. You look at the doughnut and your passions say, "Mmm...doughnut." Your emotions say, "Doughnuts taste good, and I want that one." Your intellect says, "You've already eaten half a dozen doughnuts today, and you're supposed to be getting *into* shape, not further *out* of it." Your will makes the decision: to have or not to have another health-defying doughnut. It is your faculty of reason, rightly exercised, that protects your passions and emotions from influencing you into making bad decisions. If your intellect has not been well-formed, or if you don't have the will to follow through on what you know to be the right course of action, you will become a slave to your passions and emotions. People who make decisions on the basis of these are people who consistently make poor decisions.

Let's apply the same principle to your sexuality. Let's say that you are on a first date with an attractive girl. Your passions say, "Mmm...woman." Your emotions say, "She's really pretty. I want her because it would make me feel good." Your intellect (if well-formed) says, "She is a person, which means she is worthy of respect, love, honesty, and commitment. I should not act towards her in ways contrary to respecting and valuing her as a person." Your will makes the decision of how to respond. Your intellect, when it makes a judgment about right and wrong, is called your *conscience*. If your conscience is poorly formed, you probably will make a bad decision. A well-formed conscience helps our will to resist making choices on the basis of impulse or emotional responses. When our conscience is sound, we know the right thing to do. Then it is up to our will to choose to love—remember that love is an act of the will—or to give into lust, the passion of sexual desire devoid of love.

This is an important concept. In one sense, over-coming sexual impurity is straightforward. It amounts to grasping and acting according to the proper purpose of our sexuality. Consider the following. Using a woman as a mere means to gratify one's own desires is the way that too many men have grown up thinking about the meaning of sex. Even treating a woman as someone a man wants to share a pleasurable experience with doesn't properly reflect what sex is meant to be. It diminishes or cheapens it. If a man starts from a flawed understanding of sexu-ality, it is easy to see how he will wind up acting in the wrong way and developing harmful habits and attitudes toward women and toward himself. God created sexual relations for a much higher purpose than self-gratifica-tion or even mutual pleasure-sharing. Rather, he created sexual relations to be an expression of a profound love: a person-uniting and life-giving form of love.

Love respects and cherishes the beloved. Sexual love includes respecting and cherishing one's partner *as a spouse*—as one's irreplaceable, unique, complementary, and permanent companion. It involves the kind of union that by its nature points to new human life, even if in any particular instance it doesn't result in new life. To engage in sexual relations for any lesser purpose than expressing a total, permanent commitment, with an openness to life, demeans the act. From this we can see why sexuality is very important and why impurity distorts it.

So far, we have focused on properly shaping our thinking about sexuality. We want to use our minds correctly to understand sexual relations and what they naturally express. This is important because we won't stand a chance in the battle against sexual impurity without a well-formed intellect and a truth-discerning conscience.

However, for most men the battle against impurity is not just a matter of having the right ideas and attitudes and then deciding to act on them. In fact, for many men—even many Christian men—the fight against sexual impurity is a difficult one. It can continue for years, maybe even a lifetime.

If all we need to do is "just say no to lust," why is it often so difficult to win the battle?

The Wound

There are physical reasons why it can be hard to give up pornography, masturbation, and other forms of impurity. For example, scientific research shows that the neurological pathways of pornography addicts are restructured by a stimulant as powerful as many drugs, altering brain chemistry and natural hormonal release. I don't want to minimize those factors. But compounding the difficulty of breaking free from impurity is usually some kind of underlying emotional wound.

In my experience, most men who struggle with sexual impurity, including sexual addiction, have an emotional connection to it. Usually it issues from a wound in their lives, and they comfort themselves with impure forms of sexual release as a way of self-medicating. The wound is usually associated with a sense of inadequacy, deep loneliness, or feeling like they are not worthy of love. Often men succumb to sexual temptation when these feelings are strong.

Consider this story. I know a man who was dealing with some marital problems. He is a good man, a good husband, and a good father. He shared his struggles with me and revealed that he and his wife had not had made love for several months. He then followed that up by saying, "A guy my age should not be struggling with masturbation." We talked for a while and as more of his story spilled out, it became apparent to me that he wasn't convinced that his wife loved him. When I brought this to his attention, he told me about his childhood, and how he grew up not being entirely convinced that he was worthy of love. His struggles with his wife were affected by his childhood wound, and as a result, he felt there was something lacking in him.

As we talked and prayed together, it was clear that his sexual impurity was rooted in this wound of inadequacy and that it was triggered when he felt rejected by his wife. He would turn to this sin as a means of soothing his own sense of inadequacy.

Our Relationship with Our Pain

This story is just one example of a man whose childhood pain was strengthening impure temptation in his adulthood. I have mentored a lot of men in this area of their lives. In almost every case, after discussing the subject of impurity, the man and I can identify a wound in his past related to the impure behavior.

Sometimes the wound is large. I mentored one guy my age who had been sexually abused as a young boy. He had never told anyone else about it, and he masturbated as a way to release the pain and shame that he felt from his experience. He needed a lot of healing from his past in order to move forward in purity. In cases like this, I recommend seeking professional help from a counselor, psychologist, or gifted spiritual director. It's important to reach out for such help to heal serious wounds of the spirit, just as you would go to a doctor or specialist to treat a serious wound to the body.

Sometimes the wound isn't obvious. Some people are experts at hiding their pain from others, sometimes for well-intentioned reasons, like not wanting to bother others with one's problems. One shouldn't share one's struggles with every person who will listen, but it's good to prudently unburden oneself to a trusted person. This reminds me of a young man I mentored who had a physical disability. He was a prayerful young man, and the way that he outwardly dealt with his disability inspired many people. He was the last person you would suspect to have had a pornography problem. When we talked about the emotion that accompanied his temptation to act impurely, he revealed that he didn't think a girl would ever love him because of his disability. He felt justified in his use of pornography because of his feelings of rejection.

In my own case, I was an insecure teenager who struggled with masturbation and pornography. I was not secure in myself and had no firm identity. When I had to leave my hometown and relocate while in high school, loneliness and depression set in. Masturbation became a way for me to banish my feelings of loneliness.

Consider what Deacon James Keating, Ph.D., says about men who turn to sexual impurity to console the pain of their own inadequacies or festering emotional and psychological wounds:

> Unhealed erotic movements of the will become enslaved to immediate and artificial consolation. It is a consolation that looks to relieve, through physical pleasure, a host of painful emotions (self-hate, loneliness, anger, fear, grief, boredom) that remain unrelated to the Paschal Mystery. The relief sought in masturbation only returns compounded sadness, and a horrifying habit of choosing more and more what satisfies less and less. If this habit of entering misguided pleasure is not healed, then the man enters a cycle of shame that increases in force. Thus the [man] becomes vulnerable to a deadening despair born in self-made aloneness. This despair increases

cynicism toward life, goodness, and "the woman" (Gn 3:12, 20; Jn 19:26; Jn 2:3–5). The "healing" occurs as the wound is acknowledged, the lies are unveiled, and the light of Jesus's love reveals the Truth. This divine love has to be received into a man's wounds so that it can alter the external behavior from within. Defining the struggle for chastity is often a deep pain that is at the root of inappropriate behavior, a pain that needs healing, not numbing.[10]

Sadly, many men will never shake their attachments to impurity because of their deep emotional connection to it. They turn to pornography, masturbation, or other forms of sexual impurity as a way to numb the pain in their own lives. When this pain is triggered, much like the way emotions are triggered by watching a commercial, they medicate themselves with poisons posing as pleasurable escapes from reality.

The temptation to run away from problems by indulging in impurity may start as a child or a teenager by feeling an "innocent curiosity" regarding sexuality or as a reaction to puberty and changing hormones. But it can persist if it becomes a way to cope with pain, loneliness, and inadequacy.

In order to truly defeat lust and develop the capacity for love, a man must identify and treat the wounds in his life. This will free him to stop using destructive ways of escaping the pain.

If any of the following sounds familiar, you know you have a problem (and likely a wound) that you need to address now, before it becomes ever more deeply rooted and harder to root out as you grow older:

- You can't stop looking at porn/masturbating/ fornicating, *etc.* And why should you, anyway? Relieving sexual desires is good and natural.

- Intense emotional pain won't go away until you masturbate.

- You are inadequate.

- Women don't find you attractive and never will.

- No one loves you.

- You are doomed to be alone forever.

Until these lies are uprooted and replaced with God's truth, we can't know freedom, and we never will be able to understand fully and experience God's love and plan for our lives. Uprooting the lies usually involves identifying and healing the wound that the lies attack.

Trust in God

Most of us are familiar with the story of Adam and Eve. God told them not to eat the fruit of the tree of knowledge of good and evil, but the serpent tricked Eve, and she ate it anyway. Eve then gave the fruit to Adam, and the rest is history. At first glance, it would appear that everything started with the serpent and Eve, but I would argue Adam had a significant part to play in this story. Or rather, he didn't play his part.

In Genesis 2:15, the Bible states that God took Adam and put him in the garden to till and keep it. You might think this means nothing more than Adam being a gardener, but this is not the case. Yes, Adam had responsibility for "tending" the garden. That is, of making creation "fruitful." But this responsibility included protecting it. When the Bible says that Adam was to "keep" the garden, it uses the Hebrew word *shamar*, which can also be translated as "to guard" or "to protect." Adam was given the responsibility of protecting the garden. But what did he need to protect it from? One answer is disorder. Gardens need protecting from weeds and overgrowth. Adam's work included making God's creation fruitful by tilling it but also protecting it from the harm of disordered growth. As we shall see, though, physical disorder was not the only thing from which Adam was to protect the garden. Moral disorder—sin— was also a threat. Which brings us to the serpent.

Most of us have heard the story of the serpent entering the garden. We might be inclined to think of an ordinary garden snake. But this misses a subtle point about the serpent. The word used in Genesis to describe the serpent is the word *Nachash*. It does mean *serpent* but it can also refer to a dragonlike sea serpent, who represents evil, which is opposed to God's purpose. When Genesis refers to the cunning serpent, ancient readers would have thought of more than a little snake. Behind the serpent they would have understood there to have been a greater being at work to undermine God's will for man and woman.

The serpent addresses the woman and begins by planting doubt in her mind: "Did God say, 'You shall not eat of any tree of the garden'?" (Gn 3:1). The serpent is twisting the truth because God actually said they could eat from *every* tree of the garden, except the tree of the knowledge of good and evil, which would lead to death (Gn 2:17). When Eve corrects him, the serpent sows further doubt, "You will not die. For God knows that when you eat of it your eyes will be opened" (Gn 3:5). He implies that God is not trustworthy. He claims not only that God is lying, but that he's doing so to keep Adam and Eve from the good of having their eyes opened. After her exchange with the serpent, Eve disobeys God and eats the fruit. What's more, she gives the fruit to Adam who also succumbs and disobeys God (Gn 3:6).

Interestingly, some scholars argue that Adam was with Eve the whole time the serpent was addressing her. The use of the plural form of "you" (Gn 3:1, 4–7), which we miss in the English, implies Adam was there with Eve. In other words, Adam could have protected the garden and Eve by trying to drive out the serpent. Or he could have intervened to stop Eve from eating the fruit. Instead, he did nothing, showing his own doubts about God's trustworthiness.

I remind you of this story because it demonstrates one of the ways temptation works in the area of lust. When our pain is triggered, we can start to think that we're in pain because God is holding out on us. That if only we disobey him and give in to impurity, then we can be happy. Like Adam and Eve in the face of trial, we can start to question God's love for us and wonder if he's keeping something good from us. Like Adam failing to live according to God's calling, the heat of the moment can reveal we don't trust that God has something better than what the temptation offers. If we're going to walk the path of sexual purity, it is crucial that we drive out the lie that God wants less for us than we want for ourselves. He actually wants more and better for us than we could ever want for ourselves! This belief is indispensable if we're going to choose the promises of God over the illusory and short-lived "happiness" of sexual impurity.

The Second Discipline: Writing

At Mass, after we recite the "Our Father," the priest implores our Lord to keep us "free from sin and safe from all distress." Indeed, Jesus wants to help heal our wounds and save us from our sins. But it is difficult to ask him to heal a wound if we don't know what our wound is or where it is located. We may not even be conscious of having a wound because we covered it up so long ago that we have forgotten about it, and yet it festers still.

In the last chapter, we discussed the discipline of daily prayer. Lust and impurity are nearly impossible to conquer without a relationship with God, and daily prayer is essential to forming such a relationship. The second discipline that I want to consider is the discipline of chronicling your life, by keeping a journal or penning an autobiography. Many men do not like this sort of introspection. It requires time and attention to self-reflect—to discern one's thoughts and feelings, to ponder one's past and figure out how it has shaped who one is today—and then to put it in writing. If you get into the habit, though, I bet you will be amazed at the things you begin remembering: buried treasures to cherish as well as skeletons hidden in the closet of the soul that need to be cleaned out and put to rest.

Writing is a key that unlocks many doors of the heart. And it can require fortitude: A lot of people would rather hide from themselves than know themselves. Writing is a proven method of coming to truly know the good, the bad, and the ugly about oneself and to confront that fullness of truth. The other option is to continue engaging in escapism, which lends itself to sin. Too many men seem to have an escape pod of one kind or another, whether it's sexual impurity, alcohol or drugs, food, professional sports, celebrity worship, video games, music, unsocial "social" networking, you name it. The question is, what are you escaping from that's making you do things that block the way to becoming the man God made you to be?

Every time you are either tempted to lust in your heart or commit an act of impurity, I want you to stop and examine your thoughts and feelings. See if you can identify a lie that you are telling yourself or a common feeling that you are having at times of temptation. When you identify something, write it down in a journal or notebook. Keeping a log will be helpful as you learn to identify the wound.

It may be helpful to add the following simple prayer to the daily prayer routine I pray you've been developing:

Jesus, please help me to identify and name the wound that is in my heart. Pour forth your grace on me and lead me to healing. Amen.

Conquering lust and impure acts is, as we have said, going to be a battle, and it will be helpful to identify what drives your enemy in battle. As Jesus said, "What king, going to encounter another king in war, will not sit down first and take counsel whether he is able with ten thousand to meet him who comes against him with twenty thousand?" (Lk 14:31). Before entering the battle, we have to study our opponent. Sexual impurity is not the only enemy. Perhaps the greater enemy is the emotional wound attached to the impure behavior. In order to overcome this enemy, we need to know our enemy. The act of naming something is powerful. Journaling can help us do so. You also may consider the larger, revealing, and liberating act of writing out your life story from your earliest memories through the present. Try writing one page covering each year of your life, then see where that leads. You might be astonished how writing can illuminate so much of your life.

Chapter 6

Entering the Battle

Jesus performed miracles throughout his public ministry, many more than Scripture records. It is no secret that healing the wounded and afflicted was a big part of his mission. My favorite miracle story is that of Jesus healing a blind man named Bartimaeus (*cf.* Mk 10:46–52). Bartimaeus was begging on the side of the road when he heard that Jesus was walking by. He began shouting, "Jesus, son of David, have mercy on me!" Apparently he caused quite a commotion, because people started trying to hush him. He shouted even louder, "Son of David, have mercy on me!" Jesus stopped and asked him, "What do you want me to do for you?" He responded, "Master, let me receive my sight." Jesus replied, "Go your way; your faith has made you well." Immediately, Bartimaeus could see.

I love this story because of Bartimaeus's persistence and his ability to identify his wound (not that it was hard in his case). He knew who Jesus was, and Bartimaeus recognized the opportunity to change the course of his life with Jesus's help. He would not take "no" for an answer. If only all of us pursued Christ's healing with the same persistence. Another reason I love this story is because of the question that Jesus asked. He asked what Bartimaeus wanted. *And Bartimaeus knew exactly what he wanted.* Bartimaeus wanted to see.

As we saw in the previous chapter, men will fail in the battle for purity because they don't know who their real enemy is. They fail to identify their wound. It is not merely a battle to overcome lust by exercising self-control. It is a battle to understand ourselves, our desires, and how we view ourselves. Bartimaeus was healed of his blindness because he was able to name his wound and ask Jesus for specific help. Jesus spoke, and Bartimaeus was healed.

When we know our wound, we are then able to present the wound to Jesus for healing. Healing is possible. It can even happen in the blink of an eye. All that is necessary is for Jesus to speak the word, and we shall be healed. But how is it possible for Jesus to heal us, and how does it work?

The Holy Spirit—the Healer

When God created the world, according to the opening of Genesis, his Spirit moved across the primordial "waters," while the earth was said to be "without form and void" (Gn 1:1). This was an ancient way of describing the nothingness from which God brought forth creation. The Hebrew word used for the Spirit in this text is *ruah*, which also means wind or breath. This is the same word used throughout the Old Testament for God's Spirit as well as for the spirit of man. The point is, the Spirit of God was present and operative when God spoke the world into existence. God said, "Let there be light" (Gn 1:3), and there was light. God commanded various aspects of creation to come to be, including human beings, and they came into being. Both the Spirit of God and the Word of God were involved in creation.

In the New Testament, we also see the power of God's Word as well as his Spirit. St. John's Gospel begins with a prologue, which in some ways parallels the creation narrative in Genesis. "In the beginning was the Word, and the Word was with God and the Word was God," John 1:1 declares. "[A]ll things were made through him and without him, was not anything made that was made" (Jn 1:3). St. John goes on to state, "The Word became flesh and dwelt among us" (Jn 1:14). This means the Word of God—Jesus Christ—is a divine Person and that divine Person created the world and took on human form to live among us, fully human and fully divine. According to John 1:12, "[T]o all who received him, who believed in his name, he gave power to become children of God…" Later, Jesus speaks of people being born anew, of water and the Spirit (*cf.* Jn 3:3, 5, 8). In the work of God in our lives, we have both the Word of God and the Spirit of God.

If you have ever studied Trinitarian theology, you know that the Father, the Son, and the Holy Spirit are in a perfect and eternal loving communion with one another. The Blessed Trinity is three divine Persons who possess the one divine nature. The Father loves the Son, and the Son loves the Father, and their love is so real and perfect that it is a distinct Person in and of himself, the Holy Spirit. We cannot say that the love between the Father and Son creates a third Person (like a husband and wife procreate a baby) because the Holy Spirit shares in the divine nature, which is eternal: meaning that he can have no beginning or end and therefore can't be conceived in time. To put the matter succinctly, we can say that the Holy Spirit is the Perfect Love of the Father and the Son.

Why go deep into theology? So that we might understand why Jesus Christ, who is the Word made flesh, can, by the power of the Holy Spirit, heal your wound. When Jesus heals someone, whether physically, emotionally, or by forgiving his sins, he does so by loving him back into health through the action of the Holy Spirit. He pours the Holy Spirit upon him—the same Holy Spirit who is the love of the Father and Son. The Holy Spirit was active in the creation of the world, and he is active in our "re-creation" as children of God through Baptism and in our continual process of conversion throughout life. Many think of conversion as a once in a lifetime event, but conversion simply means a "turning back," which for us means turning back to God whenever we fall into sin. The Holy Spirit was working within Bartimaeus as he called out to Jesus. And since Jesus is the Word of God, he can merely speak the words, "Go your way; your faith has made you well" (Mk 10:52), and Bartimaeus receives his sight. This is why we echo the words of the Roman Centurion at Mass when we say, "Only say the word and my soul shall be healed" (*Roman Missal*, 26). By the power of Jesus's word and the working of the Holy Spirit, souls as well as bodies can be healed.

Holy Spirit in Battle

You might still be wondering how the Holy Spirit will figure into our spiritual battle plan. For illustration, we can look to Scripture to see the battle-hardened Third Person of the Trinity in combat time and again.

When the Egyptians pursued the Israelites to the Red Sea, Moses told the Israelites, "Fear not, stand firm, and see the salvation of the LORD, which he will work for you today; for the Egyptians whom you see today, you shall never see again. The LORD will fight for you, and you have only to be still" (Ex 14:13–14). Moses then led the people to the waters, stretched out his hand, and a strong wind (*ruah*) parted the Red Sea (*cf.* Ex 14:21). Christians see this as the Spirit of God "moving across the waters" once again, as at the time of creation. We know the rest of the story. The Israelites passed safely across the Red Sea, but when the Egyptians pursued them, the waters came crashing down upon them. The Israelites were delivered from their enemy that day.

Many readers will know the story of the Israelite judge named Samson. God gave Samson great strength, and he was a fierce warrior. Scripture tells us the story of Samson slaying one thousand Philistines with the jawbone of an ass in retribution for killing his wife and family (see Jgs 15). This story has epic movie thriller written all over it. Before Samson defeated his enemy, "The Spirit of the LORD came mightily upon him" (Jgs 15:14). It was the Spirit of the Lord who led Samson to victory.

Most people also know the story of David and Goliath. David was a young shepherd boy who defeated Goliath with his sling and a well-placed stone to the giant's forehead. That small David volunteered to take on the Philistine army's fiercest warrior in one-on-one combat when everyone else in the Israelite army cowered in fear is a testament to his courage and faith in God. In defeating Goliath, he delivered Israel from the Philistines. You can read the story in 1 Samuel 17. How did David accomplish this feat? You guessed it: the Holy Spirit. One chapter earlier in the first Book of Samuel, we encounter the story of how the prophet Samuel anointed David in his hometown of Bethlehem. After the anointing, the Bible says, "And the Spirit of the LORD came mightily upon David from that day forward" (1 Sm 16:13).

The greatest example of the Holy Spirit leading to victory in battle concerns Jesus himself, but it was a spiritual battle. St. Matthew's Gospel recounts Jesus's baptism in the River Jordan by St. John the Baptist. When Jesus was baptized, the heavens opened up, and "he saw the Spirit of God descending like a dove...and behold, a voice from heaven saying, 'This is my beloved Son, with whom I am well pleased" (Mt 3:16–17). Scripture goes on to state that "Jesus was led up by the Spirit into the wilderness to be tempted by the devil" (Mt 4:1). So, the Holy Spirit descended upon Jesus at his baptism, and he immediately led our Lord into battle with man's oldest adversary, whom he overcame by resisting three temptations of the Evil One.

What can we learn from this? If you are going into a battle, you want the Holy Spirit with you. It is the difference between victory and defeat. As the Bible shows time and again, God will deliver you from your enemy through the power of the Holy Spirit, who will also give you the faith and courage to confront your foe.

The Third Discipline: Engaging the Holy Spirit in Prayer

When most people pray, they fall back on prayers that they learned as a child. This is fine in the beginning, but we need to mature in our prayer lives in order to realize its full potential. Prayer is supposed to be an intimate conversation with God. Prayer can also be directed to God through intercessors such as the saints, especially the Blessed Virgin Mary. To realize the full potential of prayer, it's important to learn how to pray in the power of the Holy Spirit.

It is the Holy Spirit who will replace the lies in your life with truth. It is the Holy Spirit who will help you identify your wound and heal it. It is the Holy Spirit who will provide strength for the battle and the weapons necessary to win (even the jawbone of an ass, as in the case of Samson, or a sling and a stone, as in David's). If you are going to win the battle against sexual impurity and become a man of God, you need to pray for the *empowerment of the Holy Spirit.*

Here is how to begin. Every day, for the rest of your life, you should pray:

Come, Holy Spirit. Come into my heart. Rush upon me with your power and your grace. Reveal and heal my wounds. Mend what is broken, comfort what is hurting, and speak truth into my heart where I have accepted lies. Empower me with the gifts of the Spirit that I may become that man that you have created me to be. Only say the word and my soul shall be healed. Amen.

Pray this prayer every day. In fact, write it down in the journal I hope you've started. Write it down right now, before you forget. Persevere with it. Take the words to heart and go forward in faith, day by day. If you do, change will begin happening in your life. As you pray, listen for the voice of the Holy Spirit. He may come to you in a gentle urging in your soul to confess your sins and receive God's absolution in the Sacrament of Reconciliation. He may speak to you through a conversation you have with a friend. You may hear the voice of the Holy Spirit in the quiet of your heart. Or perhaps he will speak through a Scripture verse that jumps out at you. Pray for the guidance of the Holy Spirit and you will be surprised by victories full of grace.

My Own Experience

Let me tell you about another experience I had at World Youth Day in Madrid—one far more uplifting than trying to stop that wannabe Romeo and Juliet in the throes of unpoetic passion. Oddly enough, the big events at World Youth Day weren't the ones that most affected me. There was a side event, hosted by Life Teen International, where a speaker gave a presentation, followed by praise and worship during Adoration of the Lord in the Blessed Sacrament. At that time in my life, I was wrestling with a wound of inadequacy, feeling like I didn't measure up in my vocation as a husband and father. I asked the Holy Spirit for guidance and during Adoration I heard Jesus say, in the silence of my heart,

"You are loved." Those three words were exactly what I needed to hear from God to heal a wound of my own imagining. (Real or imagined, wounds hurt and need to be named before they can be healed.)

Simple experiences with God can have huge impacts in our lives. In this case, Jesus only had to say the word, and I was healed. To find the healing words that will set you free, call upon the Holy Spirit and persevere in prayer.

The Bible is a great place to find a "word" or message by which the Spirit of God can set us free. After all, the Bible's words aren't mere human words. While literally written by human authors, they were divinely inspired to express the Word of God. Divinely inspired means God-breathed (*cf.* 2 Tim 3:16), which means the Bible truly is the work of the Holy Spirit. What's more, the Bible isn't simply words that God spoke many years ago or a mere recording of things God did. When God speaks, he speaks across time, meaning that the Word of God can speak to our own hearts today.

Here are some healing Scripture verses that mean a lot to me and have healed many wounds in my own heart. Reflect upon them. They may help you, too.

Fear not, for I have redeemed you; I have called you by name, you are mine. When you pass through the waters

I will be with you; and through the rivers, they shall not overwhelm you; when you walk through fire you shall not be burned, and the flame shall not consume you. Because you are precious in my eyes, and honored, and I love you. (Is 43:1b–2, 4a)

You will know the truth, and the truth will make you free. (Jn 8:32)

You are all fair, my love; there is no flaw in you. (Sg 4:7)

As the Father has loved me, so have I loved you; abide in my love. (Jn 15:9)

For I know the plans I have for you, says the Lord, plans for welfare and not for evil, to give you a future and a hope. (Jer 29:11)

Fear not, for I am with you, be not dismayed, for I am your God; I will strengthen you, I will help you, I will uphold you with my victorious right hand. (Is 41:10)
Cast all your anxieties on him, for he cares about you. (1 Pt 5:7)

In my distress I cry to the Lord, that he may answer me. (Ps 120:1)

Chapter 7

Dumping Your Fake Girlfriend— Overcoming Pornography

Maybe you've seen *Fireproof.* If not, I highly recommend it. It's a movie about a young, struggling married couple, Caleb and Catherine Holt. They have a big fight, and Catherine tells Caleb that she wants a divorce. At first, Caleb believes this is what he wants, too, but after some reflection he isn't so sure. Caleb is a fireman who lives by the rule, "Never leave your partner behind in a fire." With some coaching from his best friend and after following forty days of marriage exercises in a journal his father gave him, Caleb decides to give the marriage one more shot. Catherine, on the other hand, is not willing to work on their marriage, and she is cold to his attempts at reconciliation. This begins a journey for Caleb, as he discovers how to win back the heart of his wife. This journey leads him to Christ and to a personal revelation of what love is about.

It turns out that pornography was a major cause of their marital strife. This should come as no surprise: today, over half of the marriages that end in divorce do so because one partner, most always the husband, has an obsessive interest in pornography—namely, Internet pornography.[11] Caleb had become addicted to it, but thought his obsession would go undiscovered if he viewed pornography on their home computer when Catherine wasn't around. But she found out, and in the heat of an argument, exclaimed, "If looking at that trash is how you get fulfilled, that's fine, but I will not compete with it!" In days of old, it used to be actual women who were marriage-breakers. Now it's virtual women who anonymously expose themselves for the furtive pleasure of married men they never will meet. No wife should have to compete with either, of course.

My favorite scene is when Caleb works his way through the journal exercises and he is challenged to give up vices and sins for the sake of his marriage. The journal calls these "parasites" because they suck the love out of a loving relationship. Caleb had become dependent on pornographic websites in order to fill a void—his need for affection—but instead it was sucking the lifeblood out his marriage. After Caleb surrenders to Christ, however, he finds new strength and a new understanding of love.

One day, he sits down at the home computer and a pop-up screen appears, inviting him into a pornographic website. He stares at the screen for a second and is clearly tempted. But not only does he resist temptation, he rids himself of the near occasion of sin the computer poses. He grabs the machine, takes a baseball bat to it outside, and tosses what's left of the pile of junk into the trash. His wife comes home from work to discover a bouquet of red roses where the computer used to sit, along with a note that reads, "I love you more!"

With the grace of God, real-life battles with sexual impurity can have similarly happy endings.

It's Time to End Your Attachment

To win the battle against impurity, you must do more than try to stop looking at pornography. You need to take a baseball bat to a vice that has gone viral among the male population, especially in the form of Internet pornography.

God has a plan for our lives. And, for many men, he has created women who will one day be their wives. If you are called to marriage, then there is a woman who will become central to your life's mission. She is someone to pursue and to love. No other woman should be your concern when it comes to sexuality.

In the Sermon on the Mount, Jesus shocked his listeners with challenging teachings. For example, he said, "You have heard that it was said, 'You shall not commit adultery.' But I say to you that every one who looks at a woman lustfully has already committed adultery with her in his heart" (Mt 5:27–28). Jesus took the Sixth Commandment's prohibition of adultery to a new level, making the mental act of lust tantamount to the physical act of carrying it out.

Pornography cripples the heart of a man. It attaches him to a false promise of intimacy and love. Rather than uniting a man with a woman in an embrace of love, pornography creates a fantasy world where a man finds fake "intimacy" with women with whom he has no relationship. Some might say that pornography is no big deal—that they are only "appreciating the beauty of the female body." But a man who looks at pornography conditions himself to become bored with a woman's body. As he looks at websites, watches DVDs, and flips through magazines, he conditions himself to flit from one woman's body to the next, never spending more than a few seconds on each. These images of women are stripped of their personhood. The man looking at them has no idea about the fleeting object before him. He does not know her story, her hurts and pain, her hopes, dreams, or interests. Who are her mother and father? Does she have brothers? What do her family members think about her behavior? What would they think of me looking at her this way? Someone who looks at pornography simply uses a woman's body to excite his lusts in the hope of gratifying them. He never considers the person at whom he is looking.

This vice is the antithesis of true love and physically reconstructs your brain's neurological pathways so that you become accustomed to sexual arousal through graphic images rather than actual contact with women. By conditioning your heart and your mind to get into this habit, you are crippling your ability to love. If marriage is to be your vocation, then somewhere in the world God has a bride for you whose heart you are to win. She is waiting for you. But if you cripple your capacity to love, how will you find the real love and intimacy you are meant to enjoy?

I cannot tell you how often I have heard from wives whose husbands are addicted to pornography. One woman, who had been married for forty years, told me that there is no relationship left in their marriage. It was wrecked when she discovered that her avowedly

Christian husband had been picking up prostitutes and regularly masturbating. She divorced him but took him back two years later because he swore that he had changed. But he hadn't. She was willing to be intimate and frequently asked him to enter into intimacy with her, but they hadn't had sexual relations in fifteen years. Her husband was addicted to pornographic "girlfriends" and had lost desire for the real woman he was called to love exclusively, his wife. Sins of sexual impurity killed his capacity for love and desacralized the bonds of Holy Matrimony.

You would be shocked at how often this sort of narrative plays out. If pornography has become your mistress, you need to dump this fake girlfriend before she has the chance to displace the woman meant to be your true love.

Ending Your Relationship

The best part about dumping this fake girlfriend is that she isn't real, so you don't have to be concerned about hurting anyone's feelings. So how do you do it?

Remember Jesus's teaching about adultery? The problem begins in the heart, which includes how we think of women and how we look at them. Jesus provides an action plan for all who struggle with lust. He says, "If your right eye causes you to sin, pluck it out and throw it away; it is better that you lose one of your members than that your whole body be thrown into hell" (Mt 5:29). This is not "Jesus meek and mild" speaking, so we had better pay attention.

How should we interpret what he says? Is Jesus telling us to blind ourselves to escape damnation? No. Jesus is using extreme language to make an important point: that we should get rid of whatever causes us to sin, no matter how important we think it is. Caleb from the movie *Fireproof* demonstrated what Jesus is talking about. He discovered he was too weak to keep a computer in his home, at least during this time of recovery as he detached himself from his pornographic vice. For him, the choice came down either to getting rid of the computer or losing his wife, not to mention risking his soul. When you think of it that way, the choice is easy. It is as if Jesus said, "Better to take a baseball bat to your computer than to have your whole body thrown into hell."

There is a difference between what you need in your life and the things you have that bring "comfort"— things from which you might not be able to imagine parting. Ask yourself the question, "Where do I find my pornography?" Whatever you answer is what you either need to get rid of, pure and simple, or alter so that it no longer poses temptation. Consider this:

1. You don't need a smartphone. Almost every app on a smartphone is purely for luxury. A "dumbphone" allows you to text, take calls, and even check email. Every other function on a phone is largely unnecessary. Do you use your phone as a calendar? Buy a real calendar or planner. Use it for social media? Social media is not a necessary part of life. Need it for the camera? Buy a digital one. You get the idea. If you regularly view pornography on your phone, it's time to replace it with a phone that makes pornography inaccessible.

2. You may or may not need a personal computer, at least one with an Internet connection. If you don't need one, get rid of it. If you need one for school or work, here are a few helpful tips. Have your computer in a public place, such as the living room or kitchen. You are less likely to look at pornography if you keep the computer out of your bedroom. You also might install software such as Covenant Eyes (www.covenanteyes.com) and/or X3 Watch (www.x3watch.com). Covenant Eyes records every site you access, then compiles

a regular report sent to your designated "account-ability partner," such as a parent, priest, or close friend who knows you struggle with pornography and will hold you accountable for wherever you wander in the World Wide Web. X3 Watch blocks pornographic sites.

3. If you have a subscription to any pornographic magazines, cancel it. Now. If you have pornographic materials in your possession, destroy them. Don't just throw them away, lest someone else comes across them.

4. If watching certain movies or television shows leads you to sin, stop watching them. So many movies and TV shows nowadays make a joke of impurity or else glamorize it. Don't underestimate their influence. If the television remains a source of temptation, stop watching it altogether. You're not necessarily ending your relationship with television for the rest of your life. But like Caleb and his computer, you may have to step away from it for a while because you may not be a totally free man just yet. You need to control television and all electronic devises instead of being controlled by them.

5. Music. Sexually suggestive music saturates our culture. Good music can uplift the soul, but bad music can drag it down. Don't let the latter happen to you.

These suggestions can be difficult steps to take, but they may be necessary if you want to become the man that God has made and called you to be. The world is in great need of real men. Become one. It's not enough to go part way. You have to take a baseball bat to your sexual vice or addiction. So dump the fake girlfriend and take the next step to freedom.

The Fourth Discipline: Protecting Your Eyes

So far, we have considered the disciplines of daily prayer, knowing oneself through writing about oneself, and praying to the Holy Spirit. If you practice these three disciplines each day, then God can work with you to help cleanse you from impurity within. This is the internal work associated with overcoming impurity. The disciplines we will cover in the next several chapters belong to the external work you can do.

This chapter's discipline is learning to protect yourself from "lust of the eyes" (*cf.* 1 Jn 2:15–17). This used to be called practicing "custody of the eyes." When you look at something, you imprint an image of it onto your mind. Lust begins in the mind, with a thought turning into a temptation, and a temptation encouraging action. Your mind will use the images residing there to lead you into lust. In this way, every impure image you've ever seen can become food for the ever-hungry monster of lust inside your mind. Feeding it will only make it more ravenous. Starving it will make it become weak and easier to defeat.

When you first cut yourself off from pornography, the images you remember will try to draw you back into the pornographic habit. This may even drive you a bit crazy at first because you've conditioned yourself to use those images to draw you into imaginary sex. Don't fear: This feeling will pass in time. As you go without pornography, the images in your mind will fade and you will think of them less and less. When an image does pop into your head, say a prayer for that woman and ask the Lord to remove permanently that image from your mind. Eventually, when you are completely free, you will hardly remember the images of the women that you once looked at. I know this to be true because this was my experience.

Protecting your eyes means more than just cutting yourself off from pornography. Sadly, many women dress immodestly as a way to get men's attention, even if they protest to the contrary or aren't fully conscious of it. There are also immodest magazine covers at the grocery store, lewd television commercials, billboards with suggestive images, and lots of other sources out there to assault your eyes with impure images. You can't avoid them entirely, but there are ways to diminish greatly their influence.

One technique that I find helpful in avoiding lust of the eyes is the practice of "bouncing your eyes." This means that when your eyes fall upon a lustful image, you immediately look away before you allow that image to be imprinted on your mind. This is an easy habit to develop. It's as simple as looking the other way. It also will help you exert more control over your thoughts so that when you look at a woman, you can see the person, not just the body.

The eyes are the window to the soul. By this expression, people usually mean that we can see into someone's soul, or inner self, by looking deeply into his or her eyes. Here, though, it means that the eyes can allow light or darkness to penetrate our souls. The pornography monster lives on the darkness within a man's soul. There it feeds on the images the man chooses to see. To conquer the monster, he must starve the beast. Protection of the eyes is an important tactic to achieving purity and the victory of freedom for your soul.

Put a Face on It

Pornography can seem a victimless crime but in fact it claims many real victims, not just you and, say, your future spouse. Most men never consider how much the pornography industry abuses women. Many pornography "actresses," when given the opportunity to tell their story, speak about the times when they have cried, been beaten, been raped, and been in pain on set. The industry has no compassion for these women. This merciless industry treats them just the way that you would expect: They are used and then cast aside when their selling point—their beauty—fades.

Recently, there was a story about a young woman who performed in pornography to pay her way through college. An article in a prominent magazine tried to paint it as a success story: an empowered and sexy woman using pornography to better herself. However, a documentary revealed that she was anything but empowered. She spoke about how her sexual experiences had aged her far beyond her real age, eighteen. She said she carried a tremendous amount of emotional baggage for a woman her age. She told a terrible story about crying on set because she was forced to have sex with a fifty-year-old actor or lose her job. This story about someone's "little girl" was heartbreaking.

I tell this story to make you consider the person behind the image or movie. As you journey to freedom, you will face a significant temptation to return to pornography. Browsing the Internet, you may even encounter a pop-up putting you face-to-face with a pornographic image. If this happens, look at the woman's eyes and not her body. Imagine she is someone's daughter and someone's sister. Imagine her life, and how great her pain and struggles must be. Put a face on the image, but don't dwell on it. If you stay on the website, you contribute to untold human suffering. You are the person these websites are trying to draw in, so click away from the pop-up. Don't support a life damaged by performing in pornography.

Other Resources

There are many tremendous resources available to help you free yourself from pornography. (If you don't have a problem with it, but know someone who does and wants help, please let him know about these resources.) I already mentioned those two software programs,

Covenant Eyes and X3 Watch. You may also wish to consider the following:

- The Porn Effect (www.theporneffect.com). This website provides facts about pornography as well as inspiration and practical steps to help overcome an attachment to it.

- *Victory* by Matt Fradd and Mark Hart. This booklet provides a step-by-step walk-through on how to end a pornography addiction.

- Catholic Answers (www.catholic.com) offers *Porn: 7 Myths Exposed* and *Delivered*, both by Matt Fradd. *Delivered* recounts real-life stories of men and women who escaped from the prison of impurity to freedom.

- Lighthouse Catholic Media (www.lighthouse catholicmedia.org) offers several excellent CD recordings about pornography by eminent Catholic speakers, including: *The Hidden Battle* by Matt Fradd, *Detox* by Jason Evert, and *The Pornography Plague and the Path to Christian Purity* by Jeff Cavins.

Chapter 8

Self-Mastery over Masturbation

At the Catholic school I attended when I was growing up, the topic of human sexuality was specially addressed every year. Our teachers, who were probably more uncomfortable with the subject than the students, would muddle through the textbook and pray that the students wouldn't ask hard questions. I first heard about masturbation in the fifth grade. All I remember was the teacher telling us that it was a person having sex with himself, that it was a sin, and that you shouldn't do it. At the time, that answer was good enough for me, and no one ever brought the subject up with me again.

After hitting puberty, I quickly discovered that my Catholic education in the area of human sexuality was woefully inadequate. No one had ever explained to me *why* masturbation was wrong, and as a result, I was an easy target when I hit puberty. I didn't see anything really wrong with it, and, at the time, I didn't think I was hurting anyone.

This may be your attitude toward masturbation. After all, many people in our culture encourage it and even tell you that it is healthy. But I think every person has some shame when it comes to masturbation. A priest once told me that the most difficult sin for a person to confess in the confessional is masturbation. The priest told me that typically a person would rather confess murdering a litter of kittens than say the "m" word.

If it is normal, as some people claim, why is there so much embarrassment surrounding it? What indeed is wrong with masturbation?

The Problem with Masturbation

Some medical experts (a term to be taken with a grain of salt) claim that masturbation is a normal part of human development. They point to studies suggesting that those who masturbate enjoy better physical health. The problem with the argument is that its premise is flawed. Masturbation is nothing more than simulated sex. Therefore, your body believes you are having sex when you are not. Sex was created by God and is good, so of course there will be physical benefits to engaging in sexual activity. But that doesn't mean the physical benefits of sexual activity should be pursued by masturbating. Nor does it mean the physical benefits of masturbating outweigh the spiritual, physical and emotional detriments. The problem with masturbation is that it conditions you to turn your sexual desires in on yourself, and, like pornography, this conditioning can have a negative impact on you and your ability to enter into a fully healthy marital relationship.

As we saw in Chapter 3, God created sex for the expression of deep, mutual, and complementary love between a man and a woman. He intended new human life to come to be through this special expression of love. He showed the kind of union he wants with humanity through the image of marital love. And he revealed the ultimate expression of this love in the relationship between Christ and his Church, which is the beginning of the kind of union we will have with God in heaven. Why is sex pleasurable? God designed it that way. Since the union of sexual relations is an image of the union between God and his Church, then the delight, desire, and culmination of sexual love is an image of the bliss of heaven itself.

Most of us who have masturbated did so because we discovered the powerful pleasure associated with the sexual act. But that pleasure was designed to be shared in a mutually self-giving way. It's intended to be the conclusion of an act of a self-giving, other-cherishing union between a married couple. The act of masturbation is inherently *selfish* because there is no act of love associated with it. There is no other person with whom one's sexual activity is shared and with whom one is united. Masturbation divorces sexual expression from an act of love. Masturbation is the antithesis of conjugal love. By conditioning yourself to treat sexual expression as a selfish act, you damage your ability to engage in the sexual intimacy that is supposed to be reserved for your future spouse. You condition yourself to think that sexual relations are meant to satisfy your own desires, rather than to be a gift of self to your beloved. The sin of masturbation is different from that of pornography, but the result is the same: Both cripple your capacity to love.

The Battle Against Masturbation

We've used the image of a battle for the struggle to overcome impurity. Now we can shift things a bit and think of that struggle as a war. In a war, there is usually more than one battle. So perhaps it is better to think of the effort to defeat masturbation and pornography as two separate battles in the war on impurity.

Pornography is in some respects a different kind of conflict. With pornography a man battles influences and images outside himself. He tries to prevent pornography from reaching into his soul and planting its flag therein. Masturbation is a different kind of monster. It involves a man conquering a temptation to abuse his body. The battle is more immediately internal, although it obviously can be triggered by external factors. The battle against pornography may be won by avoiding pornography and all those other external pulls toward impurity which bring on temptation, such as sexually suggestive music, movies, and literature. The same strategy does not apply to masturbation, however, since the temptation is internal and you cannot, strictly speaking, avoid your own body.

Perhaps you tried to stop masturbating but found it hard to stop. Here's at least part of the reason. If you've made masturbation a habit, then the longer you go without masturbating, the more your body starts to feel crazy, and the temptation to engage in sexual activity surges. This is because every sexual act releases large amounts of dopamine and testosterone into your body. If you masturbate regularly, your body has become accustomed to these hormones and has adjusted to create more testosterone to accommodate the frequent release of the hormone. When you stop masturbating, your body's testosterone levels build up, creating the increased temptation to release the hormone. This is why, if you have regularly masturbated and you stop for a week, you may feel like you are going to lose your mind. I have never been a cocaine addict, but I would imagine there are some similarities. You have to get this out of your system and allow your body to readjust, and it can be hellish getting there.

This is bad news, but like all news, it doesn't stay on page one for long. The good news is that your body eventually adjusts and the increased temptation will subside. And as you acquire self-mastery, the ability to say no becomes ever more easy.

Masturbation can be more difficult to conquer than pornography because the bodily adjustment you must make is often more difficult. It can take up to forty days fully to purge yourself and feel that you can manage the temptation without much distress. Within eighteen months of being masturbation free, however, you hardly notice the temptation at all. If you are going to try to detox, so to speak, the first week will be difficult, but the third week is often the make-it-or-break-it point. I share this with you so you will understand that the struggles you initially face eventually will pass. Most men who habitually masturbate, unfortunately, never make it past the first couple of weeks of detoxing because they find it too difficult to deal with the temptation. They do not understand that the temptation will subside, or if they do, don't want to endure the struggle to overcome it. But becoming a real man, pure in body and mind, is worth the effort.

The Myth of Sexual Repression

I have heard people say that refusing to give into your sexual desires and not masturbating will create a "sexual-repression complex." If you "suppress" your sexual desires and emotions, so the myth goes, your psyche will become twisted and you will develop perversions of desire that may lead to you committing sexual crimes. This myth is usually perpetuated by people who have tried to remove sexual impurity from their own lives and failed because they found that stopping was too difficult. They justify giving up by telling themselves that it is unhealthy to stop masturbating. They have convinced themselves they will become sex offenders if they stop masturbating.

This idea couldn't be further from the truth. Almost all people who give up pornography and masturbation will tell you that they have never felt better and have never once desired to do something that would make them sex offenders. Mastering your sexual desires is a virtue—it's the virtue of chastity. People who commit sexual crimes are not sexually repressed; they have become saturated in sexual impurity for so long that they no longer can tell the difference between the fantasies that they create in their minds and the reality in which they live. They commit sex crimes because they want to live out a fantasy. A study conducted by Dr. William Marshall revealed that 86% of rapists were addicted to pornography and 57% were attempting to imitate a pornographic scene they had viewed.[12]

I think my friend Jason Evert, a well-known speaker and author on the topics of chastity and theology of the body, puts it perfectly when he gives this example: Imagine that you are watching a television show with some friends and your broadcast is interrupted by a news report of a police chase. The criminal that the police are chasing is a violent sex offender. You and your friends watch as he is chased down and captured by the police. In watching this scene play out, you wouldn't say to your friends, "Boy, that guy must have seriously repressed his sexual desires. If only he had a good woman, this never would have happened. Who has a sister? I bet we can hook the two of them up on a date and his problems would be solved." It would be ludicrous to think this way.

Conquering your sexual desires in the way we've discussed will lead to freedom, not repression. Practicing self-control is about growing in virtue and your capacity to love both yourself and others—including your future spouse, if marriage should be your vocation.

Winning the Battle of Self-Control

Conquering masturbation is a winnable battle, but you will need some weapons in order to do it. St. Paul says, "Put on the whole armor of God, that you may be able to stand against the wiles of the devil... stand, therefore, having fastened the belt of truth around your waist, and having put on the breastplate of righteousness, and having shod your feet with the equipment of the gospel of peace; besides all these, taking the shield of faith, with which you can quench all the flaming darts of the Evil One. And take the helmet of salvation, and the sword of the Spirit, which is the word of God" (Eph 6:11, 14–17). In addition to having put on "the whole armor of God," as St. Paul says, you also must identify the field of battle–those places where you are most frequently tempted to masturbate, like in the shower or in your bed at night.

Next, consider the weapon you will wield in battle. St Paul refers to the sword of the Spirit, which is the Word of God. For me, this was a prayer that I would recite or recall whenever I felt the temptation to masturbate. It might be a particular Scripture passage that speaks to your heart or a prayer to a saint that is particularly effective. Whatever your weapon is, you need to have it memorized so you always are prepared for battle. The prayer should bring your attention back to Jesus Christ, who loves you beyond measure and died for your sins. It should be a prayer that reminds you of God's love for you and of your need to stand up and be a man. In the early stages of your battle with masturbation, you may find that you use this prayer very, very frequently. This is good. Just as if you were to engage in a real sword fight, the more times you strike your enemy, the more he will suffer and the fainter his return blows will become until he surrenders or is cut down for good.

The third step is to go into battle with a plan. If you frequently fall into sexual sin in the shower, don't stop showering. But take the briefest shower possible to do what a shower is for—get physically clean, not morally dirty. Make it a two or three-minute shower. (If you don't think this is possible, consider that sailors on submarines used to be given only thirty seconds to take a shower, and not even every day. Yes, it can be done.) Set a timer and race the timer. If you fall into sin in your bed, go through a prayer ritual before you get into bed where you bless your bed with Holy Water and pray for your deliverance from this sin. Always have your weapon (your memorized prayer) ready for battle and confront each conflict one at a time. If you feel the temptation to masturbate when you begin to wake up, don't just lie there, indulging temptation: Hop out of bed and start your day with a bolt of courage and a quick prayer. The important thing is that you score a victory over temptation. With each battle that you win, you will gain more and more confidence in your ability to conquer this sin.

The Most Powerful Weapons

Some weapons are more powerful than others. One of the many beautiful things about Catholicism is that our Church teaches us to tap into the intercession of the saints. Just like you would ask a friend to pray for you, the Church recognizes that those who are in heaven are not dead—they are forever alive in glory with God. By asking them to pray for us, we are asking those who are already close to Christ in heaven to intercede on our behalf for special graces. Some of the most powerful weapons that I have found when battling sexual impurity are prayers to the saints—three in particular.

St. Joseph

St. Joseph was entrusted with both the protection of the Blessed Virgin Mary and the responsibility of rearing and protecting the Christ child. When he learned that Mary was pregnant, he knew that he wasn't the father, but he trusted God's plan. He protected the Blessed Virgin even when socially that was not acceptable. When Herod sent soldiers to Bethlehem to kill all the firstborn male babies and infants, St. Joseph took his family and fled to Egypt to save Jesus (*cf.* Mt 2:13–15). He protected and provided for the family that was entrusted with the divine plan for the salvation of the world. You can imagine that Satan constantly wished to attack the Holy Family. It is with good reason that one of the titles for St. Joseph is "Terror of Demons." If Satan came after St. Joseph's family, St. Joseph went on the attack. St. Joseph is a model of manhood and a model of fatherhood. You are a member of God's family, and, if you invoke St. Joseph's intercession in any prayer, you will find that he battles hard against the temptations that seek to ruin your soul.

St. Michael the Archangel

There are many, many angels in heaven, but the Bible names only three. Tradition tells us that when Lucifer started his rebellion in heaven, St. Michael the archangel cried out, "Who is like unto God?" (the very meaning of his name, *Misha'el*, in Hebrew). The Book of Revelation picks up the story, describing how St. Michael led the armies of God's angels to victory over the fallen angels and cast them out of heaven and into hell. When battling temptation, it is a great help to call on St. Michael to protect you from evil and to help you conquer your temptation. In the late nineteenth century Pope Leo XIII was inspired to write a prayer to St. Michael, which all the faithful are encouraged to pray. If you don't already know this shorter version by heart, write it down in your journal and pray it often. It's one of the most powerful weapons you can have in your spiritual arsenal:

St. Michael the Archangel, defend us in battle; be our protection against the wickedness and snares of the Devil. May God rebuke him, we humbly pray: and do thou, O prince of the heavenly host, by the power of God, thrust into hell Satan and all the evil spirits who prowl about the world seeking the ruin of souls. Amen.

Our Lady

I could write an entire book on the importance of having devotion to the Mother of Jesus, the Blessed Virgin Mary. Suffice it to say, if you want to grow closer to Jesus, grow close to his Mother. There is no spiritual hero throughout Catholic history who did not have a devotion to Mary. She is the most powerful saint in heaven, and she labors greatly for the salvation of souls. Her importance in the story of salvation is prophesied as early as Genesis 3:15 and is alluded to throughout the Old and New Testaments, including in the Book of Revelation, the final chapter of the story of salvation. In the Old Testament, the wife of the Israelite king was not the queen. Kings usually had many wives, and the throne of the queen could not be shared. The king, however, only had one mother—and *she* was the queen of the kingdom.

The Blessed Virgin Mary is the Mother of the Son of God and, therefore, inherits the Kingdom of God as the Queen of Heaven and Earth. She is the commander of the angels of God and she sits at the right hand of Jesus in heaven. If you want to battle sin and impurity, go to the one creation of God who was most pure and fall into the arms of your heavenly Mother. Prayers to Mary are some of the most effective prayers in overcoming temptation. In particular, I strongly recommend the Rosary. I never go anywhere without my rosary, and I try to pray it daily. Frequently, I even fall asleep with my rosary wrapped around my hand.

The Fifth Discipline: Fasting

Fasting is an important spiritual discipline to incorporate into your life. On one occasion, Jesus' disciples failed to cast a demon out of a woman. When they presented the woman to Jesus, he had no difficulty in casting out the demon. The disciples asked him why they had failed. Jesus responded, "This kind cannot be driven out by anything but prayer and fasting" (Mk 9:29).

Fasting is not just a physical act, but a very effective form of prayer. When we fast, we take the suffering of the cross that we are carrying and, in the name of Jesus, we offer that suffering to God as a prayer of reparation—that is, a sacrifice to make up for or "repair" our sins and the sins of others. This we do in imitation of the ultimate prayer of reparation: Jesus' suffering and Death on the Cross, in which he offered himself up as a sacrificial Victim to repair the bridge between God and man that had been broken by sin. This form of prayer has tremendous spiritual value and merit because we are sacrificing on behalf of others. It also serves a personal, practical purpose in the quest to overcome masturbation. When we deny ourselves food or luxuries, we exercise and strengthen the will. This practice detaches us from the things of this world and helps us to regain control and the capacity to make good moral decisions rather than being puppets of impulsivity.

I want you to consider fasting on bread and water one day a month and offering that suffering for your freedom and the freedom of other men from any attachment to masturbation. (If you no longer have an attachment to masturbation or never had one, then you can pray for your continued freedom from this or any other sin.) Fasting on bread and water for twenty-four hours is uncomfortable but it will not kill you. Even if you can't do bread and water, consider strengthening your will by giving up a luxury—like dessert, coffee, television, or chocolate. Even such small sacrifices can pay big dividends: For exercising the will to any degree strengthens the spirit, making it ever easier to control your thoughts and actions.

Online Resources

There are some excellent online resources that provide help and encouragement in mastering the virtue of chastity, particularly as it pertains to masturbation. I would recommend:

- Jason Evert's *Chastity Project* (www.chastityproject .com). Jason has a tremendous number of resources and articles that encourage a person growing in the virtue of chastity.

- *Reclaiming Sexual Health* (www.reclaimsexualhealth .com) is another great website that gives the brain science behind masturbation and pornography.

- *E5Men* (www.e5men.org) is dedicated to encouraging a community of men to make monthly fasts on bread and water as a prayer for their future or current wives. This website will provide support to you in acquiring the discipline of fasting.

Chapter 9

Establishing Pure Relationships

One of my favorite things to do in my spare time is to watch a good movie. I love going to the movie theater to catch a premiere or cuddling up with my wife on the couch and watching a new release on Netflix. There's something magical about watching a good story develop on screen. If you notice, in every movie, there is almost always a love interest or a love story. Even if it's not necessarily romantic love, there is some sort of love such as brotherly love among soldiers in war or players on an athletic team.

Movie producers know that telling a truly good story on screen must engage love at some level, because the greatest desire of the human heart is love. A movie without love might impress an audience because of its cinematic brilliance or empty-headed comedy, but it will not engage the audience on a deeper—a heartfelt—level.

Our hearts relate to stories of love because our hearts desire to love and be loved.

One of my favorite love stories of recent memory is the *Twilight Saga*. This is a series of books converted into five films. The movies and books are extremely popular, in large part due to the huge teenage audience. I enjoyed the movies but not for reasons you may think. I loved the *Twilight Saga* because it very well may be the *worst and dumbest love story ever written*.

The Wrong Ways to Start a Relationship

Every good love story has a conflict that prevents two people from fully realizing their love for one another. In *Romeo and Juliet*, Shakespeare tells the story of a boy and a girl who fall madly in love with one another, but, as a result of a longstanding feud, their families do not want them to be together. The story centers on the lovers' struggle to overcome family obstacles so that they can be together forever. Of course we know the tragic outcome.

The Twilight Saga is about the love between Edward and Bella, two teenagers in high school. But there is a hitch: Bella discovers that Edward is a vampire. So, while Bella loves Edward, and Edward loves Bella, Edward also has a nearly uncontrollable desire to drink Bella's blood. This presents a real obstacle to their relationship. At one point Edward breaks up with Bella for her own good and protection. Bella handles this like any teenage girl dating a vampire would—she cries a few tears, and then she goes berserk. At one point, she actually throws herself off of a cliff because she misses Edward so much. (She survives.) As the story progresses, Edward realizes that Bella loves him so deeply that he must turn her into a vampire for her own "good," so that they can be together forever.

This is not, shall we say, a healthy way to advance a loving relationship. In fact, this isn't love at all—it's emotional dependency. Love is not all about feelings; at its core, it's not about feelings at all. Love is an act of the will: *Love wills the good of the other.* It isn't love if we attach ourselves to another person in the hopes that that person will bring us happiness, regardless of the harm the relationship may cause the other person. This is utilitarian—using another person like a tool to suit our own purpose—and utilitarian love is a contradiction in terms. It is selfish, whereas the essence of love is self-giving.

The *Twilight* notion of love calls to my mind what I like to call "the middle school relationship." If you can think all the way back to middle school and recall the "dating" relationships, you may laugh out loud. The relationships tended to consist of boys and girls coming together in some sort of awkward dialogue between friends and "dating" because they "liked" each other. This would go on for several months until one of them would decide that he or she no longer liked the other person—maybe that person no longer was fun to be around or useful in some way—and they would break up and sometimes never speak to each other again. And then on to the next crush...

Sadly, many young adults—and older ones, for that matter—still approach dating with something of a middle school mindset, which tends to give too much weight to fleeting feelings and passing interests. It's a mindset that suffers from immaturity and a limited understanding of love.

In our dating culture, we have lost our way. There are many couples that are living in a *Twilight Saga* relationship or in a middle school relationship. Neither one of these approaches is a recipe for finding real love. I want you to establish wholesome relationships with members of the opposite sex so that you one day, God willing, can forge a relationship with the right woman—a relationship that will meet the pure desire for love that both of you have.

In order to establish pure relationships, allow me to offer some proposals.

Principles for Pure Dating Relationships

Whenever I mentor young men and women in the area of romantic love, I like to share with them some of the principles that I learned when I was dating my future wife. Following are five principles that I encourage every person who is seeking real love to live by. And lest there be any confusion, I would like to make clear that I am considering dating relationships here, not mere friendship activities that members of the opposite sex might do together. The nature and purposes of these two kinds of relationships are quite different, though romantic love relationships between couples can—and often do—blossom from mixed circles of common friends. With that in mind, here we go:

1. Every relationship ends in one of two ways.

Usually, a dating relationship eventually ends in marriage or in a break-up. Few couples date for thirty years, although of course people may have long-term friendships that aren't dating relationships. If you know that the person you are dating is not the one you want to marry, then you should end the relationship. The conclusion is inevitable, and delaying it for any reason can set the stage for a bitter ending. It also does an injustice to your girlfriend if she doesn't know that you believe there's no romantic future for you together. In short, *be a man when it comes to your dating relationships*: that is, be honest, prudent, forthright lest feelings be needlessly hurt, and loving, which means willing her good. Keeping this principle in mind will lead you to raise your standards for the kind of person you date. It also helps clarify the purpose of your relationship, which ultimately boils down to discerning marriage.

2. Your dating relationship is not the most important relationship you will ever have.

Every marriage relationship ends when either spouse dies. At the moment of death, you will meet the Person for whom you were created and with whom you will hopefully spend the rest of eternity—Jesus Christ. A dating relationship should build up your relationship with Jesus, not pull you away from it. Prayer in your relationship is one of the most important things you will ever do as a couple.

3. Never make big decisions in a state of spiritual desolation.

This is a principle of St. Ignatius Loyola. It means that important decisions in your life, such as who you date, let alone marry, should not be made when you are at a spiritual low. Most all of us go through such periods in life, sometimes repeatedly, varying in degree of intensity and duration. They are not fun, but God allows them to happen for a reason. They are tests of faith that offer the potential for personal growth that would not have been possible if our path through life were one long and sweet walk with Jesus. They demand that we persevere in trust. Properly engaged, periods spent in the spiritual wilderness often precede periods of great and momentous growth. First the test, then the reward. In short, if you are in the wilderness and you don't know where God is trying to lead you because you cannot hear him just now, then you shouldn't be making important life decisions. You should be praying a lot, seeking good counsel, and in the process, finding out just what kind of man you are now and might be called to become later.

4. It's OK to be single.

Seriously, it is. Love finds us in God's time. When you date with purpose, you tend to date fewer people, but for longer periods of time.

5. Chastity is necessary for love.

When a person has not learned to master his sexual desires, but is instead mastered by them, his desires tend to be selfish. Selfishness and love are two things that do not go together. Chastity dictates that you love a person so much that you will the good for them. Practicing chastity—and protecting the chastity of others—is a requisite of all Christians, but the form of chastity depends upon their walk of life. If you are not married, chastity means abstaining from all sexual relations. If you are married, chastity means sexual relations within the lovingly exclusive marital bond. For sexual relations are proper to marriage alone because it is only in marriage that you give your entire life and self to the other person. When a man and woman give their *bodies* to one another before giving their *full selves* to another in the Sacrament of Matrimony, they are living out a lie from which a host of ills can flow.

Establishing Pure Relationships

Conquering impurity in our lives can be a difficult journey, and being in a relationship with a person while you are battling serious sexual impurity is not recommended. If you struggle with pornography and masturbation, and you are currently dating someone, it is going to be more difficult to overcome those problems. If you are currently dating someone you can't imagine marrying and starting a family with, then you should end the relationship. It will be easier for you to overcome your impurity if you are focusing entirely on that issue and don't have the extra temptation of trying to be pure with a girl.

If you are dating someone you truly love and care for, and you do not wish to end the relationship, but you have been sexually active with that person, then you need to have an honest conversation with yourself and your girlfriend. Will you and your girlfriend commit to a life of chastity with one another? Are both of you committed to working to establish chastity in your relationship? If not, you may need to separate for a while so that you can work on the virtue of chastity apart from one another. This will allow you to return to one another free of attachment to sin so that you are truly able to love each other as you both deserve.

Making decisions like these is not easy. It can be even harder when you are sexually active with a girl. Your emotions and sexual attraction can cloud your judgment. Still, regardless of your feelings, if you are not committed to one another in marriage, you shouldn't be doing things with your bodies that say you are. That amounts to lying to each other. You may have deep feelings for one another. You may truly care for one another. But if you haven't committed your lives to one another in marriage, you don't love each other in the way people who have sexual relations with one another should. As my friend Jason Evert says, "The problem is not that you are going too far, it is that you are not going far enough." Don't simply give your body to a girl and take her body as your own. Give your whole life to that girl. Commit to her, in front of her friends and family and God himself in the form of a lifelong commitment. Promise her security; promise her you will love and provide for your future children. Promise her you will take care of her when she needs hip replacement fifty years from now. That is the love that she desires and to which you are called. If you are in a sexual relationship without giving her that, then you are lying to her (and she to you). If you are not ready to enter into a marriage relationship and to make that kind of commitment, then you are not ready for the responsibility of sexual relations.

We've discussed the problems pornography and masturbation may cause for future relationships. Sex outside of marriage can be an even worse foundation for your long-term future with your beloved. Sexual involvement can distort a couple's perception of each other. It is not a pure act of love, and down the road—even if you do end up marrying—your relationship certainly will not be stronger because of those bad decisions, but very well may suffer because of them. Make a decision now to live for the kind of love for which God created you—the kind of love you truly desire. Make a commitment only to have pure relationships. That decision will prepare you to make the right choices later on.

How Far Is Too Far?

It is absolutely true that vulnerability and intimacy are requirements of any loving relationship. In dating relationships, you need to discover the appropriate level of physical and emotional intimacy that reflects the current state of your relationship. If you are dating, having sex does not express the love that you feel for one another.

That action should only be shared by couples who are in a lifelong commitment of love in marriage. However, holding hands and warmly hugging one another may communicate the affection that you have with the one you are dating. Also keep in mind that acts of love may be wonderfully expressed in ways that don't involve any physical contact, such as gifts, acts, words of kindness, and all those acts of chivalry that used to be taken for granted (holding doors, helping your date out of the car, giving her your jacket on a chilly night). These are things that separate the men from the boys.

A good gauge for appropriate behavior is keeping your girlfriend's father in mind. Consider that the person in a young girl's life who is tasked with the primary responsibility of protecting her is usually her father. A father is generally protective of his daughter, and for good reason. He has protected, provided, and cared for her throughout her life. (Indeed, the bond between a father and "daddy's little girl" is very important, and girls without good and strong fathers often suffer relational problems later in life when it comes to men. Remember the opening story about Mikala?) There is a reason why a father gives his daughter away at the altar, because he is handing off that responsibility to the man that she will marry. A man, if he is a good father, naturally feels a sense of urgency to protect and provide for his daughter.

If you want to know where the line is when it comes to going too far, ask yourself the question, "How would I react if my girlfriend's father walked in on us together? Would I be embarrassed? Would I feel a need to run and hide?" Or could you proudly stand in front of him and demonstrate that your actions are loving toward his daughter and not pushing the limits with her? A good indication of what is too far is usually easily gauged by imagining the father's reaction: Would he shake your hand or throw you out of the house? Always consider this when you are in the presence of your girlfriend. She is protected by her father, and you need to honor your girlfriend and her father by not doing anything of which he wouldn't approve.

The Sixth Discipline: Setting Boundaries

If you are going to enjoy a pure relationship, then you are going to need to set boundaries. If you are currently dating someone, then you should plan on having a conversation with her to set very clear boundaries of what you will and won't do in a relationship. These boundaries will act as principles in your relationship to protect and guard both of you from making mistakes that would harm your growing love. By protecting one another from lust, or from entering into a sexual relationship before you've made a lifelong commitment, you are creating an atmosphere of love and respect for one another.

If you are not in a dating relationship, make a list for yourself and share this list of principles when you enter into a future dating relationship.

Your boundaries should be specific and both you and your girlfriend should agree upon these principles ahead of time. (If she won't agree or takes the whole matter too lightly, this should set off relational alarm bells. If you are not on the same plane of moral maturity, you probably should call it quits now before things get complicated. Pray to the Holy Spirit for guidance, especially the gift of wisdom and the virtue of courage.) An example of some boundaries might be:

1. Only closed-mouth kissing.

2. No kisses lasting longer than a few seconds. Be warm, not passionate.

3. No contact with areas of the anatomy intended for procreation or child rearing.

4. No sitting on beds together or spending time alone in one another's bedrooms.

5. The lights always stay on.

6. No sitting alone in a parked car.

Boundaries should never be made or set with the other person when you are in the heat of passion. That is a recipe for failure. Once you are aroused, you are not going to want to set boundaries that throw a wet towel on your passion. So, set your boundaries ahead of time and make sure that you don't compromise. Real men have strong principles and don't compromise on them.

Other Resources

To learn more about setting boundaries to keep relationships pure, I recommend the following resources:

- *How to Find Your Soulmate Without Losing Your Soul* by Jason and Crystalina Evert

- *How to Save Your Marriage Before Meeting Your Spouse* by Jason Evert, a CD recording available from Lighthouse Catholic Media (www.lighthouse catholicmedia.org).

- The myriad of resources available at Jason Evert's *Chastity Project* (www.chastityproject.com)

Chapter 10

What to Do When You Fall

As you wage war against sexual impurity, you will likely not win every battle. When you succumb to temptation and sin, it is crucial that you embrace God's mercy and seek his forgiveness through the Sacrament of Reconciliation. As Catholics we confess our sins to God through a priest and ask for God's forgiveness and for reconciliation with Christ and his Church. The Sacrament of Reconciliation can be intimidating because confessing one's sins aloud, however liberating, is something one doesn't tend to look forward to doing. Yet it is extremely grace-filled and beautiful, and the more often you go, the more battle-ready you will become. In fact, this Sacrament is so powerful that it can be life-changing.

One day in college, I was standing in line waiting for the next available priest for Confession. I was feeling particularly fragile that day and was hoping to get a compassionate priest to hear my sins. Nervous, I swallowed hard, and went to the next priest available. When I was done confessing, I looked up at the priest and awaited what I feared might be a scolding. I'll never forget what happened because it was the most powerful experience I have ever had in the confessional. Father Thomas looked me right in the eyes, and I saw the eyes of Christ. It was like he was looking right into the depths of my soul. I've never experienced a look like that before or since that Confession. He gave me some very compassionate and pastoral advice, gave me my penance and absolved my sins. I left there experiencing both a spiritual and emotional change in my heart.

Why the Sacrament of Reconciliation?

Jesus summarized the Ten Commandments in two statements: love God and love your neighbor (*cf.* Mk 12:28–31). When we sin—no matter how "private" the sin may seem—we sin against both God and neighbor. While sins vary in severity, every sin that we commit injures our relationship with our neighbor and injures our relationship with God. Some sins, called mortal sins, are such grave violations that they rupture our relationship with God to the point of imperiling our salvation. (To learn more about the nature and types of sin, see the

Catechism of the Catholic Church, 1847–1876.) Yet in his mercy and love, God is willing to forgive all of our sins, even mortal sins. And while Jesus could have chosen to forgive our sins in many different ways, he decided to do so person-to-person.

All throughout the Gospels, Jesus forgives people of their sins, a power he handed on to his Apostles. After he rose from the dead, he appeared to the Apostles in the Upper Room and said to them, "Receive the Holy Spirit. If you forgive the sins of any, they are forgiven; if you retain the sins of any, they are retained" (Jn 20:22–23). In turn, the Apostles passed on this power to the bishops who succeeded them, who in turn conferred it on their priests, a process that has continued to the present day. This is why we go to a priest or bishop for the forgiveness of sins: not because it's a Catholic invention, but because this is how God wants us to do it. In the Sacrament of Reconciliation, you are reconciled to God through a priest acting in the Person of Christ, who is perfect God and perfect man. This Sacrament is both personal and intra-personal—since our sin affects God and neighbor, the Sacrament reconciles us with both God and neighbor. And by acting in the Person of Christ, a priest or bishop gives the penitent the soul-satisfying certainty that his sins truly have been forgiven by God himself. This spares a person a lot of anxiety—imagine merely praying for forgiveness, but left wondering if your slate is really clean—and is yet another sign of God's immeasurable love for his children.

Confessing your sins, especially sexual sins, can be very difficult, though people often make it harder on themselves by thinking that their sins are somehow unique and shocking. Priests usually have heard it all before, and there's nothing new under the sun, anyway. Confessing our sins, especially if we find ourselves repeatedly confessing the same ones, requires us to admit our errors and inadequacies, learn humility, and hold ourselves accountable for our behavior with the firm purpose of amending our ways. We must take our act of contrition to heart and avoid those things that lead us to sin; the grace of Confession will help us do so. Your confessor also can mentor you in your struggle, giving you encouragement as well as advice on how not to commit the same sins again.

So what exactly is sin and what makes it mortal? According to the *Catechism*, "Sin is an utterance, a deed, or a desire contrary to the eternal law....It is an offense against God" (*CCC* 1871). Lesser or venial sins don't automatically jeopardize our souls, but they are important to confess and avoid especially since, habitually committed, venial sins can dull our consciences and lead to mortal sins. For a sin to be mortal sin, three criteria must be met: 1) the sin must be grave matter, 2) there must be full knowledge, and 3) there must be complete consent (*CCC* 1857–9). We should avoid mortal sin at all costs because it "results in the loss of charity and the privation of sanctifying grace, that is, of the state of grace. If it is not redeemed by repentance and God's forgiveness, it causes exclusion from Christ's kingdom and the eternal death of hell, for our freedom has the power to make choices for ever" (*CCC* 1861).

You can use the three criteria above to help determine if you committed a mortal sin. This is especially relevant because sexual sins are grave matters. They abuse a gift of God intended for the love of a man and a woman in marriage: the kind of total, mutual, self-giving love by which new human beings are brought forth. Our sexuality is not something we should take lightly, nor should sins against it be considered trivial. In this morally confused culture we're living in, many people have poorly or wrongly formed consciences when it comes to sex. They may be sinning gravely without even knowing it. Such unintentional ignorance can reduce or possibly remove their guilt because the condition of full knowledge isn't met (*CCC* 1860), but other consequences and fallout from the sin remain. You, however, cannot claim ignorance, at least not any longer. If you're reading this book, you know the truth about human sexuality and should want to live accordingly in order to find complete freedom. As for the third criterion, consent must be "sufficiently deliberate to be a personal choice" (*CCC* 1859). The Church even recognizes that factors such as "force of habit acquired" can lessen the moral culpability of masturbation by hindering complete consent (*CCC* 2352). Nonetheless, hardness of heart doesn't diminish one's free will and our focus should not be on lessening culpability but rather breaking free from the bonds of sexual impurity and living virtuously.

If you commit a sexual sin along this journey of purification, the most important thing you can do is immediately repent and beg God's forgiveness, then go to Confession as soon as possible. You shouldn't presume you can always repent sometime later, since we never know the day or the hour when we breathe our last. And we must not lie to ourselves that we're not really jeopardizing our salvation by committing a sin the Church teaches to be grave matter, but we don't think is such a big deal.

One last point: If you have committed a mortal sin, you should not receive the Eucharist until after you have gone to Confession. Receiving our Lord in a conscious state of mortal sin is a very serious sin in which no graces are received. As *The Code of Canon Law* instructs, "A person who is conscious of grave sin is not to ... receive the body of the Lord without previous sacramental confession unless there is a grave reason and there is no opportunity to confess; in this case the person is to remember the obligation to make an act of perfect contrition which includes the resolution of confessing as soon as possible" (*CIC* 916). We need to remember that receiving Our Lord in the Eucharist, "body, blood, soul, and divinity," is a privilege, not a right.

Starting Over

For most young men who have not yet mastered chastity, the question of falling into sin is not a matter of *if* but *when*. Habits of sin—vices—are not easily unlearned. It can be demoralizing and difficult when you fall. You may get down on yourself and feel like giving up the fight.

I have three words to say to that: Don't give up!

Every fall should be a learning experience. It gives you an opportunity to identify the wound in your life and to pray within the pain of that wound. It presents an opportunity for you to experience God's love and mercy in the Sacrament of Reconciliation. It helps you to identify your vulnerabilities, so that you learn to guard yourself better next time. It helps to strengthen you, so that you are fiercer the next time you enter into battle. If you keep battling, if you don't give up, and if you keep praying through the wounds and the pain, you will one day be free of this sin. Victory is possible. When you fall, don't lose heart: In wars, the winning side usually has lost some of the battles along the road to victory.

For me, the war was won by fighting one battle at a time. In the midst of temptation, being chaste for the rest of my life seemed impossible. Yet when I decided to take each temptation as it came, I said to myself, "I am going to beat this one temptation." This gave me confidence, and I began winning more battles than I lost. As a result, I gained even more confidence. I won more and more battles until, one day, I found that I no longer was enslaved to habits of impurity. It wasn't that temptations never came again; it's that I knew I could beat any temptation because I had done so before.

The Seventh Discipline: Accountability

It is possible to overcome sexual impurity without the help, love, and support of others, but doing so makes it unnecessarily difficult. Jesus sent forth the Apostles "two by two" (Mk 6:7) because he knew that we do better and are stronger when we live in relationship with others and enjoy friendship, intimacy, and accountability.

This chapter's discipline is to find someone who can hold you accountable to your commitment to chastity. It could be your parish priest in the confessional, a spiritual director, or a friend who shares your beliefs and wishes to support you in your journey to chastity. Think about a person in your life who could hold you accountable and ask that person to be your accountability partner. Once you find an accountability partner you are comfortable with, begin to set up regular meetings with this person to help you on your journey to chastity.

A good accountability partner should do the following:

- Speak with you often and encourage you in the virtue of chastity.

- Protect the password for any porn-blocking software you might acquire or, in the case of Covenant Eyes, be the one you designate to receive reports of all the websites you've visited.

- Agree that you must check-in with him immediately should you be sorely tempted or have surrendered and sinned sexually.

A good accountability partner will go a long way in helping you to become a chaste person. Sometimes people try to avoid their accountability partner after they have fallen because they don't want to admit they have sinned. If you find yourself in this situation, this is an indication you need to call him. It will require some humility, but will help you get up and win the next battle.

Chapter 11

The Unmentionables

It doesn't seem like a day goes by without hearing about another sex crime on the local news. If you want an unwelcome surprise, "google" the number of registered sex offenders in your area. There's probably one quite close by.

Whether it is rape, sexual assault, voyeurism, hacking into celebrity iCloud accounts and stealing nude photos, or any other sex crime, there is no doubt that our culture has a problem with distorted, aggressive, and criminal sexual behavior. The number of people convicted of sex crimes is shocking. What makes someone go from fantasy to criminality?

When I struggled with sexual impurity, I noticed an impulse to look for different thrills as I gave into lust in the privacy of my own world. Because sexual impurity ultimately doesn't fulfill us, we remain empty inside. This leads some people to go deeper into impurity and perversion because, well…they're bored. They haven't found the intimacy they crave, but they won't break away from the sexual impurity that is preventing intimacy, so they dive more deeply into the sea of sexual perversion. Desire turns into action for such people as they seek yet a greater "thrill."

Of course not all desires become actions and not all bad desires are equally bad. Nevertheless, we should be concerned about our evil desires, especially a category of desires I call the unmentionables.

In a decade of ministry with men, I have found them willing to share, even if reluctantly, their struggles with pornography, masturbation, sexual promiscuity, and infidelity. But never has a man opened up about having disordered desires. Often this area of a man's heart and mind is *classified*. It contains things *unmentionable*, taboo. As we explore this subject, I want to be clear that I don't regard all of the topics labeled as unmentionable to be equally wrong. Some are worse than others. What they share is that they all are desires to do things contrary to God's purpose for sexuality and men tend not to discuss them with other men. In some instances, the desires involve physically harming others. In other cases, it is a moral issue only. I don't mean to offend people by grouping the unmentionables together; I realize the differences among them.

Same-Sex Attraction

First off, let me say that I'm no expert in this area. This is a sensitive topic in our culture today, and I don't set out to offend men who carry the cross of being sexually attracted to other men. Please presume my good intentions. I am also aware that some people are offended by the term *same-sex attraction*, preferring another term such as *gay* or *homosexual*. I use the term same-sex attraction because it's an objectively descriptive term that includes all those who have ever experienced sexual desire for someone of the same sex. A term such as "gay," on the other hand, generally is used for those who self-identify with their same-sex attractions.

The Church's teaching on homosexual behavior, versus a sexual inclination toward the same-sex, has been clear and consistent over the ages. Same-sex *attraction* is not sinful, while homosexual *behavior* is sinful because it opposes natural law by closing off the sexual act from the gift of life.

Despite the mainstreaming of homosexuality in our culture, same-sex attraction remains a daunting struggle for many men who have this inclination as well as a desire to be chaste. For many of them it is a source of pain and confusion that doesn't lend itself to being openly talked about. For these men especially, it is an unmentionable desire of the heart.

It will help to make a distinction at the outset. Having experienced a sexual desire for someone of the same sex does not automatically mean a person is same-sex attracted in general. Young men in puberty and even later in their teens can experience such an attraction as part of their sexual development. When you are young, most of your relationships and friendships with your peers are with members of the same sex. As you hit puberty, your attitude toward the opposite sex changes, and you begin to desire more (and different) relationships with girls. These opposite-sex relationships are primarily driven by the newly emerging sexual drives tied with physical and psychological growth and your growing desire for love and intimacy.

The thing is, puberty isn't like a light switch. Most young men don't one night go to bed having close friendships with members of the same sex and then wake up the next morning with sexual desires for the opposite sex. It happens sometimes, as a young man develops physically and emotionally, that he experiences a vaguely romantic affection for a close friend of the same sex. This feeling is usually fleeting but it can confuse a young person. It usually ceases as hormone increases ease and the body and mind continue to develop.

Another important distinction is that some are what can be called homo-emotional, referring to someone with a strong emotional desire to be around members of the same sex. This can come from an unfulfilled male relationship in a person's life—like a poor relationship with his father—that leaves a young man attracted to the very qualities he feels like he does not possess. This type of emotional attraction can lead to homosexual desire and behavior if the wound is not healed. But it is distinct from a sexual desire for someone the same sex.

This is not to say that all people who identify themselves as homosexual are simply confused and can be "cured." I bring up these examples to show that desires for members of the same sex do not automatically translate to a homosexual orientation. Feelings such as these, especially in teenagers or young adult males, need to be carefully analyzed so as to prevent them being acted on.

The Church, Chastity, and Homosexuality

Catholic teaching on homosexuality has been challenged, especially over the past decade. Often Church teaching is simply misunderstood. In part, this is because that teaching has sometimes been poorly expressed. Also, pastoral care to those with same-sex attraction has tended to be poorly carried out, when it hasn't been outright neglected. Homosexuality has become a hot button issue because of the political and cultural battles over acceptance (as opposed to tolerance) of homosexual relationships and the re-definition of marriage, which has made some Catholics even more hesitant to discuss it.

The Church does not recognize marriages between members of the same sex. The very concept contradicts reason and human nature. We have already seen that the intimate union of sexual relations points to the total, mutually self-giving, permanent, and complementary love between a man and a woman. "Complementary" here points to a kind of completion. Man completes women, in a certain sense, and woman completes man, in a certain sense. The two come together to form "one flesh" (Gn 2:24). They act as one life-giving being, each contributing something essential. Even when the sexual union of a man and a woman doesn't result in the conception of a new human being, their bodily actions in sexual union still are the *kind* of union by which new human beings come to exist.

It is also the case, as we have seen, that a man and a woman can express with their bodies the total gift of themselves to one another. This total gift of self includes a man's *potential* fatherhood made possible by his union with a woman and a woman's *potential* motherhood made possible by her union with a man. Even if that potential never gets realized, it is still there, pointing to fatherhood and motherhood. Two people of the same sex cannot express this kind of love by their bodily union. They can't give themselves in such a way as to give the gift of potential fatherhood or potential motherhood, because their partners aren't able to bring to the union what opposite-sex partners can or represent. But it is precisely this kind of union, a total person-uniting and life-giving union, God designed to be expressed in marriage. Anything else is inconsistent with God's purpose and diminishes the meaning of sexual union.

What's more, the kind of union that brings new human persons into the world deserves to be specially honored by society, because by means of this union society continues to exist, as new members are added to it. Even when a man and a woman do not conceive

a child, their union still signifies the very *kind* of bodily
union by which human life begins and by which society
is built up. "Marriage" is the title of the special honor
society has historically given to two people who enter
into such the relationship closely linked with this kind
bodily union. Because same-sex persons can't enter into
this kind of bodily union with each other, their union
cannot be marriage and shouldn't be considered as if it
were. In fact, it is unjust to treat same-sex unions as if
they fulfill the same purpose as heterosexual marriage.

Catholics have an additional reason not to support
same-sex marriage. As we have seen, the Sacrament of
Matrimony was given to the Church by Christ, and it is
intended to express the love of God and his people, and
Christ and his Church, which is a complementary love
(*cf.* Eph 5:32). The love of God and his people is, as it
were, written into the bodies of the man and woman,
with the woman, representing the Church, receiving her
husband, who represents Christ, in an act of conjugal
love, which is a fruitful kind of union. A union between
two members of the same sex simply cannot represent
this relationship of Christ and the Church. The sexual
union, if it is to imitate Christ's love for us, must have
the capacity to be fruitful. This is why the Church is
also opposed to a married couple rendering the sexual

act sterile by contraception or surgery. Of course, some couples through no fault of their own are infertile, but they are still capable of engaging in the *kind* of sexual union by which new life comes to exist. Their being male and female still points to the reality of Christ's fruitful relationship with his Church, while same-sex actions do not. Many people may criticize the Church's teaching on marriage, but she has been consistent in her teaching and has solid reasons for what she believes and how her children are to live.

The discussion of same-sex marriage, as important as it is, is a bit of an aside to the more general topic of homosexuality and Catholic teaching, to which we now return. So, how are people to respond if they are sexually attracted to members of the same sex? Our culture tells us that people should acknowledge their attractions, accept that God loves them just the way that they are, and seek the sexual intimacy they desire. The Church teaches that people who are attracted to members of the same sex (for whatever reason) should embrace *chastity* as a means of finding the intimacy that they seek. In other words, just because God loves us doesn't mean we're free to act however we like, indulging whatever tendencies or inclinations we happen to have. We have seen this in our discussion of opposite-sex attraction and pornography.

And although God loves us as we are, that doesn't mean he doesn't love us in such a way as to call us to a better, fuller way of life. As the old saying goes, God loves the sinner but hates the sin. In fact, it isn't rare for people who once indulged in the gay lifestyle to address and heal the wounds stoking their same-sex attraction, then go on to live heterosexual lives, even finding in marriage the intimacy they once sought without success through same-sex relationships.

If a union between two members of the same sex will always fall short of communicating true conjugal love, as Christ and his Church teach, then it is unloving for two people to enter into such a relationship. And it would be unloving for the Church to treat such a relationship as if it were the same as a conjugal union. Rather, the Church invites all people with same-sex attraction to turn their attention to a deep relationship with Jesus Christ, who can help them find appropriate intimacy in their relationships, an intimacy that respects the full truth about sexual love. It is possible, through prayer and a life lived in virtue, to find deep consolation in a relationship with Jesus and filled with chaste friendships.

The Church's teaching on homosexuality is in some ways difficult but she invites us to trust in God's plan and his promise, as well as to rely on God's grace and mercy.

If you think about it, all vocations have difficulties. Marriage, too, is difficult. Husband and wives have the responsibilities of becoming one and, if blessed with children, they are given the task of rearing and educating children together. The Church invites them to entrust their fertility to the Lord and not to restrict their self-gift, which is what happens with contraception. (Such a restriction violates the meaning of the sexual union and contradicts a couple's wedding vows). This presents them with their own challenge of trusting God's plan for their marriage and family. Priests and consecrated religious make a commitment to celibacy as a means of being witnesses to the Church and giving themselves fully to Christ. They find intimacy in union with Christ. They, too, have obstacles to overcome and difficulties to face. Each vocation has a way of challenging us to become holy by relying on, and trusting in, God to meet the desires of our heart.

If you are attracted to members of the same sex, take those desires to Christ in prayer and do not be afraid to struggle with his invitation to deeper intimacy with you. Cast into the deep with Christ, and see where the journey takes you. You also might be interested learning about an organization called Courage. This international Church apostolate ministers to those who experience same-sex attraction, as well as their family and friends. The Courage website, www.couragerc.org, is an excellent resource for the Church's teaching on this sensitive subject, and for ways a person with same-sex attraction can find support and encouragement to seek virtue, reject the false allures of the happiness of the gay lifestyle, and grow in Christ's love.

Sexual Abuse

We have seen how untreated wounds often underlie problems with purity. Those who have suffered sexual abuse have some of the deepest wounds, which, in turn, can lead the victim to suffer sexual dysfunctions, disorders, and compulsions. They may use masturbation and pornography as a way of taking control over the feelings from abuse.

The first thing that always must be said when addressing sexual abuse is that it is not the fault of the abused person. He was a victim whose innocence and vulnerability were preyed upon by a disturbed, sinful individual who has jeopardized his own salvation and that of others. Recall that Jesus Christ reserved some of his harshest words for those who defile the young and innocent: "Whoever causes one of these little ones who believe in me to sin, it would be better for him if a great millstone were hung round his neck and he were thrown into the sea" (Mk 9:42). As with all wounds, Christ desires to heal this wound, and the Divine Healer is capable of healing an abused person's heart and soul and restoring what was taken. If you have been abused and haven't told another person, you should prudently consider doing so. We cannot find healing unless we let the Lord bring light to our darkness and suffering. Sunlight, as the saying goes, is the best disinfectant. A tremendous amount of healing will occur just in the sharing of your story. You also should consider speaking with a counselor who can walk you through the process of healing. Christ heals wounds, but he often works through human agents. The guidance, direction, and experience of a professional can greatly help a person to discover his wounds to bring them Christ for healing, thus preventing the horror of sexual abuse from causing even more horror later in life.

Taboo Attractions

Sex addicts and heterosexuals who act out intrinsically disordered desires may be a small minority among the world's population. But as the popularity of *50 Shades of Grey* suggests, their perversions are becoming more socially acceptable. For those who are unfamiliar with the best-selling novel, made into a popular movie by the same name, it revolves around a dashing, successful man and a beautiful woman who engage in "torture sex." The entertainment industry is making a lot of money normalizing formerly taboo sexual practices such as this, one result being that ordinary people may not feel ashamed if they practice them.

Step back for a second and think about this. If sexual relations are not simply meant to communicate the love between a man and woman united in marriage, but also are supposed to image the love between God and humanity, Christ and his Church, then "torture sex" is its antithesis. There is nothing loving about causing a person pain to derive sexual thrills. This is not a desire or practice that should ever be encouraged. So why, then, are so many people attracted to such perversions?

The trend to practice or at least fantasize about "torture sex" is a symptom of the greater sexual disorders emerging in our society. More and more men have fallen so deeply into sexual impurity that they fantasize about, or even have strong desires to act on, violent aggression in an attempt to satisfy their sexual appetites. Becoming ensnared in the lie of pornography causes men to view women more and more as means of sexual gratification, and less and less as human persons created in the image and likeness of God. In the worst cases, this may encourage men to be aggressive or stop at nothing to use a woman for their own gratification.

If you have recurring rape fantasies, practice voyeurism, or have been tempted to try "torture sex," then you should seek counseling and psychological care. Do not delay in seeking help. These thoughts and practices are dangerous for you and others.

Counseling

With any of the unmentionables in this chapter, counseling can provide great assistance and may even be necessary for you to manfully address and conquer sexual impurity in your life. Even if you don't struggle with any of the disordered desires described above, counseling can help you through the process of purification. Do not be afraid or ashamed to seek help. Many, many people seek counseling in their lives at one time or another because all of us are wounded in one way or another. And people need people. Hiding one's wounds and allowing them to fester into twisted desires and perhaps even criminal conduct is not a recipe for human flourishing.

When looking for a counselor, one should seek out a Catholic who is fully in line with the Church's teachings on sexual morality, has an authentic understanding of the human person, appreciates the motivations for becoming pure, and promotes habits of virtue and personal responsibility. Your pastor or diocese should be able to recommend counselors who meet these criteria. Another great resource is catholictherapists.com.

Chapter 12

Purity of Heart

At Franciscan University of Steubenville, where I received my undergraduate degree in theology, it's popular for students to go on mission trips during spring break. These can be domestic or international, and students learn about the various options during the annual Missions Week on campus.

When my senior year rolled around, I really wanted to take advantage of my last opportunity to go on a mission. However, I felt completely burned out. I was engaged and wedding preparations were underway. I was working on my senior thesis and completing my final course work. Also, I already was committed—overcommitted, probably—to various other ministries and activities on campus. I felt called to do a mission, but the more I learned about each different mission opportunity, the more I felt exhausted and overwhelmed. In the end, I didn't feel God's call to any particular mission, and I started thinking that I would just use spring break to rest up. But then I learned about the mission trip to the beaches of Panama City, Florida. Evangelizing *on the beach* for an entire week? I was sold.

What I didn't anticipate was the kind of impact that the mission would have on me. I thought I would get to take in the beaches of sunny Florida while sharing my love for Jesus with a few people. I didn't realize that our visit to the beaches of Panama City coincided with MTV Spring Break.

An Unexpected Lesson in Purity

MTV Spring Break is a time when college students descend on one of America's beautiful beaches for a wild week of binge drinking, sexual hook ups, free concerts, and parties. For a chaste man, MTV Spring Break is not the best place to be. Panama City's beaches were littered with mostly naked, intoxicated college girls and guys looking to hook up. Our mission trip involved sharing the Gospel message with them. I wasn't totally naïve as to what I was walking into, however. After all, our mission trip did involve some preparation.

When the mission started, two things quickly became obvious. One, evangelization and booze do not mix well. A drunk person who talks with you about God will likely—though not necessarily—forget everything you've said afterward. Two, there was big business happening at this event. Everywhere you looked, there were vendors trying to sell or promote products and services. From booths sponsored by alcohol labels, to condom distribution booths, to radio shows doing wet shirt contests, to free concerts, to bars and hotels doing promotional events—everyone was out on the beach to make a buck. How could twelve Catholic students from Ohio make an impact in this money-grubbing, hedonistic milieu? So I prayed, "Jesus, why do you want me here? What are you trying to teach me?"

On the last day of the mission, our group decided to go to the epicenter of the MTV party and walk around the beach praying and speaking with anyone who would listen. There was a moment when another guy and I ended up in front of a stage where a radio disc jockey was hosting a "booty shake off" contest with several college girls competing on stage. Each girl had one minute to "twerk" herself to victory while a raucous crowd of college guys cheered her on. It was degrading.

When the contest started, the guy who was with me said, "I don't need to be looking at this," and walked off. I understood completely. We should avoid near occasions of sin and protect our eyes. But I couldn't leave because I was struck by the contrast between how these girls were behaving and how God created them to be. It was almost a clinical experience, witnessed not through the eyes of lust, but those of our loving Lord.

I stared right at the face of one girl, shaking her behind on the stage to vulgar cheers. My heart sank for her. I saw a young girl degrading herself for attention, maybe even affection. She was made in God's image and remained precious in his sight, but was exhibiting herself like a choice cut of meat. I didn't lust for her; I felt pity for her.

As strange as it may sound, observing this human travesty made a significant impact on me. *It occurred to me in that moment that I was free.* I was able to see with the eyes of purity.

St. Paul said, "For freedom Christ has set us free; so stand fast therefore, and do not submit again to a yoke of slavery" (Gal 5:1). When I was a senior in high school, I broke away from the sin of impurity by the grace of God and by learning to practice self-control and incorporate disciplines into my daily life. But in that moment on the beach, it occurred to me that I was truly experiencing the virtue of chastity—I could see the person and love her for who she was and I could feel compassion for her because I was free of the temptation to lust after her. I was free to love.

On the beach that day, I was surrounded by so many temptations to lust. But I had no desire to lust. In every person I saw that day, I saw an unfulfilled heart and a lost soul—people just like I used to be, chasing after the next hedonistic thrill. I was no longer bound by lust. By cooperating with God's grace and working hard to become the pure man God created me to be, I was free to love.

Now I don't want to give you the impression you shouldn't avoid situations in which you may be tempted to sin or that virtuous people can never be tempted into sin. Not at all. You don't become pure and then become impenetrable to impurity. And no one should presume to stand, lest he fall. My point is that I had a graced realization at that moment on the beach. I realized what God had mercifully accomplished in me. This is why I can say to you that with grace and effort, you can break the bonds of impurity. And when you do, you will experience liberation and a self-mastery that includes the freedom to love others and to value them as persons in their own right, rather than to see them as objects for your pleasure.

Defining Chastity

You have read up to this point, and we have been on a journey together that is nearing its end. I made the plea for you to stand up and be a man—a pure man—because the world is dying for lack of us. We have learned about God's plan for sexuality and what it means to be a disciple of Jesus Christ. We have learned about our need for healing and the power of the Holy Spirit to heal our deepest wounds. We have learned to practice daily disciplines—forming habits to sever the bonds of pornography, masturbation, sexual promiscuity and other deviations from God's plan. We have learned to seek grace, forgiveness, and accountability; to accept responsibility if we fall; and if we do fall, to reconcile ourselves with Christ and his Church in the Sacrament of Reconciliation and then move onward with the firm determination to sin no more and avoid whatever leads us to sin.

If you have faithfully followed this plan, and you have diligently practiced the recommended disciplines, I have no doubt that you already have experienced a measure of freedom in your life. If your purity is still fragile, take courage: Keep taking the steps and don't be afraid to lean on someone. Seek further help if needed.

Sometimes the final step, once you have learned all of the strategies and keys to success, is simply making the firm resolution to stand up and be a MAN.

I shared the story about my mission trip to make one final point. Learning to abstain from sexual impurity and reject temptation is a big step in the journey to being chaste. But it is not the final step. The end goal is not for you to say "NO" to sex. The end goal is for you to learn to say "NO" now as a means of eventually saying "YES" to love. Sex is not bad; it is very, very good. As we mature, we should learn to control our sexual desires as a means of fulfilling our greater desire for love. This will help us express that love sexually if and when we enter into Holy Matrimony. When you are no longer a puppet of temptation and have mastered yourself, you are free to give yourself fully—physically, emotionally, and spiritually—in a lifelong commitment to the bride our Lord wishes you to marry. This is the purpose of learning to practice the virtue of chastity. Chastity is about teaching us how to love: to unite with a person to whom we give ourselves, rather than taking from a person to serve of self-gratification.

For if I don't truly possess myself, because I am ruled by my passions and desires, how can I give myself to someone else? I can't give what I don't have. Chastity enables me to give myself to another. This is why St. John Paul II said, "Chastity is necessary for love."

The Difference That You Will Make

Imagine a world where men treated women with dignity and respect—a world where men loved instead of succumbing to lust. It would be a much happier world, with practically no rape, abortion, infidelity, or divorce. The porn industry and all of its ills would disappear. Poverty would be reduced, since single mothers are the largest demographic of those living beneath the poverty line. More children would be loved, more families would be strong. A world without lust would be a much better world.

How do we get there? One man at a time. You can be part of the solution to the crisis of manhood in the world. The difference that even one man can make—a man who chooses love over lust and embraces all Christ teaches through his Church about human sexuality—will affect the lives of countless people for generations. I firmly believe that the greatest problem in our world today is a crisis in manhood. What is needed is for more men to cast off the shackles of impurity and find freedom in pursuing Christ and real love. We need men who will stand up and live for a mission and purpose greater than themselves. You are called to be such a man. For God's sake and yours—for the sake of so many others your life touches and will touch—just do it. I will pray for you as you join the ranks of those changing the world by casting off the shackles of lust and becoming a man of virtue.

Endnotes

1. John Paul II, *Memory and Identity* (New York: Rizzoli Books, 2005), 28–29.

2. Jamie M. Lewis and Rose M. Kreider, "Remarriage in the United States," American Community Survey Reports, March 2015, http://www.census.gov/content/dam/Census/library/publications/2015/acs/acs-30.pdf.

3. U.S. Census Bureau, Current Population Survey 2010, "Living Arrangements of Children under 18 Years/1 and Marital Status of Parents by Age, Sex, Race, and Hispanic Origin/2 and Selected Characteristics of the Child for all Children 2010," Table C3, http://www.census.gov/population/www/socdemo/hh-fam/cps2010.html.

4. Gretchen Livingston and Kim Parker, "A Tale of Two Fathers: More Are Active, but More Are Absent," Pew Research Center Social & Demographic Trends, June 15, 2011, http://www.pewsocialtrends.org/2011/06/15/a-tale-of-two-fathers.

5. Richard A. Friedman, "Infidelity Lurks in Your Genes," *The New York Times*, May 22, 2015, http://www.nytimes .com/2015/05/24/opinion/sunday/infidelity-lurks-in-your-genes.html?src=twr&_r=2.

6. ChristiaNet, Inc., "ChristiaNet Poll Finds that Evangelicals Are Addicted to Porn," *Marketwire*, August 7, 2006, http://www.marketwire.com/press-release/christ ianet-poll-finds-that-evangelicals-are-addicted-to-porn-703951.htm.

7. 2014 Pornography Survey and Statistics. Proven Men Ministries. http://www.provenmen.org/2014porn survey/.

8. Jason S. Carroll, Laura M. Padilla-Walker, Larry J. Nelson, Chad D. Olson, Carolyn McNamara Barry, and Stephanie D. Madsen, "Generation XXX: Pornography acceptance and use among emerging adults." *Journal of Adolescent Research* 23 (2008): 6–30.

9. Elizabeth Flock, "Devout Catholics Have Better Sex, Study Says," *US News & World Report*, July 17, 2013, http://www.usnews.com/news/articles/2013/07/17/ devout-catholics-have-better-sex.

10. James Keating, "Surrendering to the Healing Power of Christ's own Chastity." *Ignatius insight: Institute for Priestly Formation,* August 2009, http://ignatiusinsight.com/ features2009/jkeating_chastity1_aug09.asp.

11. Jonathan Dedmon, "Is the Internet bad for your marriage? Online affairs, pornographic sites playing greater role in divorces." Press Release from The Dilenschneider Group, Inc., Nov. 14, 2002, http://www.prnewswire.com/news-releases/is-the-internet-bad-for-your-marriage-online-affairs-pornographic-sites-playing-greater-role-in-divorces-76826727.html.

12. W. L. Marshall, "Pornography and Sex Offenders," in Dolf Zillmann and Jennings Bryant ed., Pornography: Research Advances and Policy Considerations (Hillsdale, NJ: Lawrence Erlbaum Associates, Inc., 1989), 185–214. Daniel Lee Carter, Robert Alan Prentky, Raymond A. Knight, Penny L. Vanderveer, and Richard J. Boucher, "Use of Pornography in the Criminal and Developmental Histories of Sexual Offenders," Journal of Interpersonal Violence 2:2 (June 1987): 196–211.

Appendix

Selected Battle Strategies

Disciplines for Battling toward Purity

Prayers for Battling toward Purity

Prayer for Freedom

Lord Jesus Christ, I pray that you would take me by the
hand and lead me to freedom from sexual impurity. I
pray that I may know you intimately, that you would
reveal yourself in my life. I pray that I may know you

better and grow closer to you every day. Jesus, I know that the journey will be difficult, and I ask that you will strengthen me for it. Jesus, I pray that you will bring to light my wounds that are attached to sexual impurity and that you will bring healing to those wounds. I pray that you will bring relationships into my life that will support my commitment to chastity. I ask you to remove relationships that pull me away from you. I pray that you will guide me through temptation and protect me from evil and selfishness. Jesus, be my teacher. Teach me to love. Teach me to pray. Teach me to be like you—to be the man that you created me to be. Should I struggle, carry me through that struggle. Should I fall, have mercy on me and lead me back to you and to your Sacraments. Guide my intentions, desires, and actions to purity and chastity. Help me, Lord, to never give up the fight and to be able to declare—for the glory of God—that I am free from any attachment to these sins. I ask this in the name of the Father, and of the Son, and of the Holy Spirit. Amen.

Prayer to the Holy Spirit

Come, Holy Spirit. Come into my heart. Rush upon me with your power and your grace. Reveal and heal my wounds. Mend what is broken, comfort what is hurting, and speak truth into my heart where I have accepted lies. Empower me with the gifts of the Spirit that I may become that man that you have created me to be. Only say the word and my soul shall be healed. Amen.

Prayer for Identifying the Wound

Jesus, please help me to identify and name the wound that is in my heart. Pour forth your grace on me and lead me to healing. Amen.

Prayer to St. Michael the Archangel

St. Michael the Archangel, defend us in battle; be our protection against the wickedness and snares of the Devil. May God rebuke him, we humbly pray: and do thou, O prince of the heavenly host, by the power of God, thrust into hell Satan and all the evil spirits who prowl about the world seeking the ruin of souls. Amen.

Memorare

Remember, O most gracious Virgin Mary, that never was it known that anyone who fled to thy protection, implored thy help, or sought thine intercession was left unaided. Inspired by this confidence, I fly unto thee,

O Virgin of virgins, my mother; to thee do I come, before thee I stand, sinful and sorrowful. O Mother of the Word Incarnate, despise not my petitions, but in thy mercy hear and answer me. Amen.

Litany of St. Joseph

Lord, have mercy. *Christ, have mercy.*
Lord, have mercy. *Christ, hear us.*
Christ, graciously hear us.

God, the Father of heaven, *have mercy on us.*
God the Son, Redeemer of the world, *have mercy on us.*
God the Holy Spirit, *have mercy on us.*
Holy Trinity, one God, *have mercy on us.*

Holy Mary, *pray for us.*
Saint Joseph, *pray for us.*
Renowned offspring of David, *pray for us.*
Light of patriarchs, *pray for us.*
Spouse of the Mother of God, *pray for us.*
Chaste guardian of the Virgin, *pray for us.*
Foster-father of the Son of God, *pray for us.*
Diligent protector of Christ, *pray for us.*
Head of the Holy Family, *pray for us.*
Joseph most just, *pray for us.*

Joseph most chaste, *pray for us.*

Joseph most prudent, *pray for us.*

Joseph most strong, *pray for us.*

Joseph most obedient, *pray for us.*

Joseph most faithful, *pray for us.*

Mirror of patience, *pray for us.*

Lover of poverty, *pray for us.*

Model of artisans, *pray for us.*

Glory of home life, *pray for us.*

Guardian of virgins, *pray for us.*

Pillar of families, *pray for us.*

Solace of the wretched, hope of the sick, *pray for us.*

Patron of the dying, *pray for us.*

Terror of demons, *pray for us.*

Protector of Holy Church, *pray for us.*

Lamb of God, who takes away the sins of the world, *spare us, O Lord.*

Lamb of God, who takes away the sins of the world, *graciously hear us, O Lord.*

Lamb of God, who takes away the sins of the world, *have mercy on us.*

V. He made him the lord of his house:

R. *And ruler of all his substance.*

Let us pray.

O God, who in thy unspeakable providence vouchsafed to choose blessed Joseph to be the spouse of thy own most holy Mother: grant, we beseech thee, that we may deserve to have him for our intercessor in heaven, whom we reverence as our defender on earth: who lives and reigns world without end. Amen.

Scriptures for Meditation

God's Word can heal wounds of the heart. Reflecting upon these verses may help you heal and find freedom.

> *Fear not, for I have redeemed you; I have called you by name, you are mine. When you pass through the waters I will be with you; and through the rivers, they shall not overwhelm you; when you walk through fire you shall not be burned, and the flame shall not consume you. Because you are precious in my eyes, and honored, and I love you.* (Is 43: 1b–2, 4a)

> *You will know the truth, and the truth will make you free.* (Jn 8:32)

> *You are all fair, my love; there is no flaw in you.* (Sg 4:7)

As the Father has loved me, so have I loved you; abide in my love. (Jn 15:9)

For I know the plans I have for you, says the Lord, plans for welfare and not for evil, to give you a future and a hope. (Jer 29:11)

Fear not, for I am with you, be not dismayed, for I am your God; I will strengthen you, I will help you, I will uphold you with my victorious right hand. (Is 41:10)
Cast all your anxieties on him, for he cares about you. (1 Pt 5:7)

In my distress I cry to the Lord, that he may answer me. (Ps 120:1)

Principles for Pure Dating Relationships

1. Remember that every relationship ends in one of two ways: marriage or break-up.
2. Your dating relationship is not the most important relationship you will ever have.
3. Never make big decisions in a state of spiritual desolation.
4. It's OK to be single.
5. Chastity is necessary for love.